BACKGROUNDS TO SHAKESPEARE

Literature and the Theater in Shakespeare's Day

Robert C. Evans

Jeffrey Moody and MeKoi Scott
Editorial Assistants

CHELSEA HOUSE
An Infobase Learning Company

Backgrounds to Shakespeare: Literature and the Theater in Shakespeare's Day
Copyright © 2012 by Infobase Publishing

Chelsea House
An imprint of Infobase Publishing
132 West 31st Street
New York, NY 10001

Library of Congress Cataloging-in-Publication Data
Literature and the theater in Shakespeare's day / Robert C. Evans.
    p. cm. — (Backgrounds to Shakespeare)
  Includes bibliographical references and index.
  ISBN 978-1-60413-524-4 (acid-free paper)
  1. Theater—England—History—16th century. 2. Theater—England—History—17th century. 3. Literature and society—History—16th century. 4. Literature and society—History—17th century.
  PN2589.L58 2012
  792'.094209031—dc23
                   2011043209

Chelsea House books are available at special discounts when purchased in bulk quantities for businesses, associations, institutions, or sales promotions. Please call our Special Sales Department in New York at (212) 967-8800 or (800) 322-8755.

You can find Chelsea House on the World Wide Web at
http://www.chelseahouse.com

Series design and composition by Erika Arroyo
Cover designed by Alicia Post
Cover printed by Yurchak Printing, Landisville, Pa.
Book printed and bound by Yurchak Printing, Landisville, Pa.
Date printed: March 2012

Printed in the United States of America

This book is printed on acid-free paper.

CONTENTS

PREFACE

The present book, like its companion volume on culture and society in Shakespeare's day, differs from many such books in that it tries to let Shakespeare and his contemporaries speak, as much as possible, for themselves. By quoting from so many primary documents, I have tried to give readers a sense not only of the thinking of the period but also of the ways such thinking was often expressed. The Elizabethans and Jacobeans were often highly memorable in the ways they spoke and wrote. Rather than merely paraphrasing what they had to say, I have tried to make their own vivid voices heard.

The sources on which I rely are taken mainly from Shakespeare's lifetime, which lasted from 1564 to 1616. I have tried to give a well-documented sense of what it was like to be involved with the theater during this period. All quotations have been modernized in their italics, capitalization, and punctuation to make them as accessible as possible to most readers. The collections of sources on which I have drawn are listed at the end of the volume. Dates cited for plays are usually those of first performances; again, I have tried to cite only play texts published during Shakespeare's lifetime.

I am very grateful to Jeff Soloway for suggesting and supporting this project. I am also thankful to Jeff Moody and MeKoi Scott for their close attention to the text and to my colleague Alex Kaufman for help on a particular historical issue. Finally, I am deeply grateful to my wife, Ruth, and to our four-legged son, Taylor, for their love and support.

All quotations from Shakespeare are from *The Riverside Shakespeare: The Complete Works*, edited G. Blakemore Evans, 1997. For a helpful listing of dates of plays, see *The Early Modern Drama Database* (http://homepage. mac.com/tomdalekeever/earlymodern.html), which assembles information from a variety of standard scholarly sources.

INTRODUCTION:
THE LITERARY LANDSCAPES OF
RENAISSANCE ENGLAND

A "REBIRTH" OF INTEREST IN LITERATURE

Perhaps the most astonishing thing about the literature produced during the reigns of Queen Elizabeth I (1558–1603) and King James I (1603–25) is how quickly it became and remained so good. Numerous significant writers all appeared in a relatively short period of time. Equally impressive is the fact that the literature of this period (called "Elizabethan" as convenient shorthand) had no especially rich native tradition to be influenced by. Geoffrey Chaucer (ca. 1343–1400), of course, was greatly admired, but he had been dead for almost two centuries. There was also a long tradition of English "morality" and "mystery" plays, but these were known mainly by memory of actual performances, since no printed texts existed. Classical writings by the Greek and Romans, especially the latter, were painstakingly studied in the grammar schools and universities, and well-written recent literature from continental Europe soon made a significant impact. Nevertheless, the literature of Elizabethan and Jacobean England seems surprisingly rich, especially when compared with the literature of the preceding 150 years.

What accounted for this sudden outburst? Partly the explanation lies in the influence of the so-called European "Renaissance" (meaning "rebirth," a term applied by later scholars). This was a broad movement, usually dated to Italy during the time of Francesco Petrarca (1304–74), whose own poetry eventually influenced most of western Europe. Petrarch (the English version of his name) was just one of many figures of his era who took an exceedingly strong interest in "classical" Greece and Rome. Of course, Greek and Roman achievements had never been entirely forgotten during the so-called "Middle Ages" (the long period preceding "the Renaissance"). Nevertheless, there is no denying that interest in the classics was especially strong during the latter period, not only in literature but in every aspect of culture and the arts.

CHRISTIANITY AND THE CLASSICS

Fundamentally, however, Western Europeans during both the Middle Ages and the Renaissance considered themselves, first and foremost, Christians.

Christianity anchored their lives to a degree that is hard for us to imagine. Religion was taken enormously seriously (so seriously that atheism was forbidden and other religions, such as Judaism, barely tolerated). Christianity was the official religion throughout most of Europe, an area often called "Christendom." Latin, the common language of intellectuals, made international communication easy, whatever the individual languages of different countries. The Roman Catholic Church, headed (often fitfully and controversially) by the pope in Rome, was the official church throughout most of western Europe. It could even be said that because of the influence of Christianity in general and the Catholic Church in particular, western Europe shared a broadly common culture—one that distinguished it strongly, for instance, from the Muslim Middle East.

The main "project" of the Renaissance, in fact, might be seen as an effort to reconcile Christianity with the best aspects of the cultures of ancient Greece and Rome. Christianity, of course, always took precedence, but during the Renaissance there was an increasing appreciation for the valuable wisdom of the Greeks and Romans (especially of their philosophers, such as Plato, Aristotle, and Seneca, to mention just a few). This wisdom of the so-called "virtuous pagans," who had often lived long before the time of Christ could easily, it was thought, be squared with basic Christian teachings. The logic was very simple: Since Christianity was the Truth (with a capital *T*), anything true in classical writings was, inevitably and necessarily, compatible with Christianity. Indeed, the fact that so many pre-Christian thinkers, especially Plato, had often come to conclusions that jibed with Christianity meant that Christianity was an eminently reasonable religion—one supported, ahead of time, by many teachings of the ancients, even if they lived well before Christ. Truth was Truth: Plato and Aristotle, using the reason God had given all humans, had discovered many truths, and all genuine truth was, by definition, compatible with Christianity.

Much truth could be discovered simply by examining the ways God reveals himself through the "book" of nature. Everything God had created revealed something about God himself. Studying God's creatures, including human beings, meant learning about God. Most human beings had to rely simply on reason to discover truths. The ancient Hebrews, however, had been granted extra insights through their long and numerous dealings with God. Christians, according to this view, were especially fortunate: They had been granted the full revelations imparted by Christ himself.

Literature and the Theater in Shakespeare's Day

DISSENSION IN "CHRISTENDOM"

Unfortunately, for centuries Christians had often disagreed about the precise nature of Christ's teachings. Heresies, or opinions that contradicted the official teachings of the Roman Catholic Church, were forbidden. Heretics were often persecuted and even killed. The Bible itself was carefully constructed in the first centuries following Christ: Some books were admitted into the official version; some were excluded as heretical; and others were either ignored or unknown. Tensions within Christendom became especially heated by the early 1500s. By that point, Christians often disagreed strongly about fundamental points of doctrine. Many were also disgusted by alleged widespread corruption in the Catholic Church. Martin Luther (1483–1546) was only the most prominent and influential of many devout Christians who eventually broke with Rome, thereby unleashing the "Protestant Reformation." Eventually "Protestants" of all sorts began to arise in Europe, especially in the north. "Christendom" was suddenly split into two broad camps, with many subsidiary splits within those camps themselves.

THE "RENAISSANCE" IN ENGLAND

All of this is important to an understanding of English "Renaissance" literature for several reasons. First, throughout the sixteenth century, England wavered continually in its official religion. Under Henry VIII (1491–1547), England was at first strongly Catholic. Then, when the Pope refused to allow Henry to divorce his first wife (who had not produced the male heir Henry desired), the king broke with Rome and established the Church of England, with himself as head. Roman Catholicism was officially abolished in England, and the vast properties of the church were seized. Catholic priests, nuns, monks, friars, and so on suddenly lost their positions, and England, along with various other nations (including neighboring Scotland), became a "Protestant" country. True and deeply convinced Protestants, however, felt that Henry's "reformation" had not gone nearly far enough. Fortunately for them, when Henry died, he was succeeded by the son he had always wanted: the young "boy king," Edward VI (1537–53). Despite Edward's youth (he was only nine when he inherited the throne), he was a devout Protestant surrounded by fiercely Protestant advisers. England seemed on the brink of a *real* reformation that would make it securely and seriously Protestant.

Unfortunately for English Protestants, the boy king soon died (at age 15), only to be succeeded by his devoutly Catholic half-sister, Mary I

Prince Edward, Henry VIII, and Jane Seymour, ca. 1545. *(detail of a larger work in Hampton Court Palace, artist unknown)*

(1516–58), who quickly began undoing many of Edward's "reforms." Mary soon married King Philip II of Spain (1527–98), the leading Catholic ruler in Europe, who now officially became King of England (although his real powers were limited by the English, who distrusted him as a Spaniard and Catholic). It was not long before Mary, in her efforts to turn England back to "The Old Faith," began to earn the nickname "Bloody Mary," by which she is still known. Protestants were often persecuted; many were even burned alive. Many people in England were still sincere Catholics, especially in the north. Yet many, in contrast, were Protestants in their hearts, if not in the allowable public behavior. Nevertheless, Catholicism seemed to have been reestablished—at least until Mary died in 1558.

ELIZABETH BECOMES QUEEN

Mary's successor, her half-sister Elizabeth I (1533–1603), was a devout Protestant, but not devout enough for some of her subjects. They wanted her to purify the church of any lingering Catholic vestiges and thus were often sneeringly called "Puritans." England was now once more officially Protestant, but it was full of people who disagreed with one another. Some were Catholics still loyal to Rome; some were Catholics who professed allegiance to the queen rather than the pope; some were conservative Protestants; some were moderate Protestants; and some were radical Protestants. Even among the radical Protestants, many different sects and sub-sects flourished. The old ideal of "Christendom"—which had probably only ever been an ideal in any case—had long since disappeared.

Elizabeth tolerated religious differences much more than her half-brother and half-sister had done. The Protestant Church of England was the official church and Elizabeth its official head. Catholicism was technically illegal, and anyone who tried to topple the official church or win converts to Catholicism might be executed. Mostly, however, Elizabeth managed to perform a difficult tightrope act throughout her reign: She managed to be a Protestant queen whom most of her ever-diminishing number of Catholic subjects could tolerate. She claimed not to want to "make a window into men's souls," and, in general, secret Catholicism was permitted during her reign, as long as it remained secret. Elizabeth had the good fortune, in some ways, of being opposed forcefully by the pope and by the Spanish king, her former brother-in-law. The pope eventually declared her assassination permissible, and Spain eventually tried to invade England (in 1588) to reimpose Catholicism. The latter effort, in particular, backfired, arousing nationalistic passions in the English and winning Elizabeth even more loyalty and admiration, especially after the Spanish were soundly and even humiliatingly defeated.

ELIZABETHAN LITERATURE

Elizabeth ruled England during a great flowering of English literature, and there is little doubt that she helped inspire much of it. Authors wrote about her, to her, and for her, but even those authors that did not mention her could flourish. During her reign England enjoyed a genuine intellectual and cultural Renaissance of its own in numerous fields, including literature, painting, music, architecture, philosophy, and, especially, drama. This Renaissance was partly inspired by the queen's own example: she was highly educated, very well read, extremely skillful in her own use of language, and genuinely interested in all the arts. She was never as generous a patron

THE UNIVERSITIES

Two of the most important institutions in Shakespeare's England were Oxford and Cambridge universities, the oldest and grandest seats of higher education in the country. Most students at these universities had traditionally trained for positions in the church, and indeed religious education was still their most important function throughout Shakespeare's era. Only males could attend, often entering in their early teen years, and increasing numbers of students did opt for university educations during Shakespeare's era. Such training was seen, more and more, as the proper achievement of an ambitious young gentleman. Many graduates became priests in the Church of England (the "Anglican" church), but many graduates also went on to secular careers, particularly in government and at court. The universities were places where religious matters were often studied and debated, and there was a growing emphasis in both universities on the kind of "humanist" education associated with "Renaissance" ideals, including rigorous training in the Greek and Roman classics and in the Greek and especially Latin languages. Other languages, such as Hebrew, were also studied, but the Christian religion as a main subject of thought and study was never far from anyone's mind during any phase of schooling during this period. Religious tensions in the country at large—especially between Catholics and Protestants, but also between conservative and radical Protestants—often manifested themselves in the universities as well. Some residential colleges within Oxford and Cambridge were known for particular religious orientations.

Powerful and wealthy people in Shakespeare's England (including the monarchs themselves) frequently took a strong interest in the universities. Often this interest took the form of endowments and other forms of financial support, and ultimately the administration of Oxford and of Cambridge was supervised by those in power at the royal court. By the end of Shakespeare's life, the universities had become even more important than they had already been in English history. University training—if not an actual university degree—was increasingly recognized as valuable experience for anyone who hoped to achieve real social status in Tudor and Stuart Britain.

"While I play the good husband at home, my son
and my servant spend all at the university."
—*The Taming of the Shrew* (5.1.68–70)

as many Elizabethan creative figures wished she were, but that was partly because she was very careful in general about money. Some people considered her stingy; she would have said she was prudent. In any case, she was surrounded by wealthy, influential people who wanted to impress her and who often shared (or at least mimicked) her tastes.

Thanks to several decades of educational reform promoted by "humanists" (a word with far more religious overtones than it tends to have today), England was increasingly literate and educated. Humanist educators emphasized knowing the classics, particularly in the so-called "liberal arts." Schools, often endowed by the wealthy, were springing up everywhere, and more and more boys (for it was mainly boys who were able to attend schools) could study Christianity and the classics, together, in the kinds of solid primary schools attended by William Shakespeare, Ben Jonson, and many other boys who eventually became leading lights of Elizabethan literature. Such schools were impressively rigorous. They often sparked a desire for further learning even in people—like Shakespeare and Jonson—unable to attend the universities in Oxford and Cambridge. Thus, two of the greatest writers of the English Renaissance, including perhaps the most gifted writer in world history, never went to college.

JACOBEAN LITERATURE

Queen Elizabeth, of course, was extremely well educated, and so was her cousin in Scotland, King James VI. Both possessed scholarly and intellectual interests and talents that would put most previous and subsequent British monarchs to shame. Thus, when Elizabeth died in 1603, having never married and leaving no heir, James's succession to the English monarchy assured a smooth transition in the intelligence of the ruler and in various other ways as well. As King James I of Great Britain (since Scotland and England were now united), James was, if anything, perhaps even more personally interested in literature and good writing than Elizabeth had been. He was not only a poet but also a theorist of poetry, and he was also the author of numerous prose works in political philosophy and theology. Literature, which had flourished under Elizabeth, continued to flourish under James. In fact, many of the best writers of the period were just as much "Jacobean" as "Elizabethan." Shakespeare wrote some of his greatest works while James ruled. Jonson, in particular, benefited from James's patronage.

One sure sign of James's strong interest in literature was his decision, almost immediately upon becoming king, to rename Shakespeare's company of actors "The King's Men." Previously they had been "The Chamberlain's Men," but now they and several other acting companies became officially connected with various members of the royal family. It became much harder for the many opponents of drama to attack acting, actors, playwrights, and theaters now that the royals had given them public sanction and support. Moreover, besides encouraging drama, James and his family also took a keen interest in promoting the writing and staging of "masques." These splendid entertainments, involving acting, music, dancing, and sometimes singing, were mostly staged at court before aristocratic audiences. Jonson became by far the most prominent masque writer of his era; he seems to have genuinely respected James and seems, in turn, to have won the personal favor of the king and of many other powerful and influential people. Meanwhile, Shakespeare's company of players performed more frequently before the royals than did any other troupe. Literature was in an even securer and officially more sanctioned position under James than it had already been under Elizabeth.

TENSIONS UNDER JAMES

This is not to say, however, that no tensions involving writers and royal policy existed during the Jacobean period. Such tensions existed under Elizabeth, and they continued under James. Inevitably, many involved religion, since religion and politics were almost inseparable. James was opposed by fanatical Catholics, some of whom, in the infamous "Gunpowder Plot" of 1605, even tried to blow up nearly the entire government. (Barrels of powder had been hidden underneath the hall where the king and most other royals would be present to open Parliament). The plot was foiled, but it left James even more suspicious of Jesuits and other rebellious Catholics. Yet James was troubled as well by Puritans—who also often happened to be enemies of actors and the theaters. James considered himself a moderate Protestant who wanted to reunite Christendom, although this goal proved impossible to achieve.

No easy generalizations can be made about the attitudes of the greatest English writers toward the reign of James. Some of the king's subjects thought he was too tolerant of Catholics; some thought he was not tolerant enough. Some thought his Protestantism was too lukewarm, and some faulted his alleged lack of devotion to the details of ruling. He was criticized for creating powerful and often unpopular "favorites" and for overspending. Many believed that his ideas about monarchy were too autocratic. Eventually such tensions and many others would lead to civil war in the 1640s, during the reign of James's son, Charles I, whose ideas were, if anything, even more autocratic than those of his father. James, however, died in 1625, and his reign was mainly one of peace, relative stability, and the flowering of an especially impressive period in British literature.

1616: A SUMMING UP

The year 1616 may be taken as an especially important one in James's reign. Shakespeare died, having spent roughly half of his life as an author writing while James was king. Ben Jonson also published a massive "folio" edition of his works in poetry, drama, and masques. No English writer before Jonson had ever before so publicly displayed himself as a *professional* author, not as a simple amateur. In 1616, too, a large folio collection of James's writings was also published. No previous monarch had ever presented his or her "works" so impressively, partly because none had ever given as much

Portrait of James I of England, ca. 1620. *(Paul van Somer)*

attention to actual writing as James had. He was a literary king in a culture increasingly and irretrievably invested in literature of all kinds.

MAJOR TRAITS OF ENGLISH RENAISSANCE LITERATURE

What, if any, were the major characteristics of Elizabethan and Jacobean literature? A good way to answer this question is to examine perhaps the most important piece of English literary theory of the era: Sir Philip Sidney's *An Apology for Poetry* (ca. 1580; first published in 1595). This is an especially significant document, not only because Sidney was almost revered (especially after his tragic early death) but also because he was such an innovative and influential writer of poems, prose, and even drama. Little in the *Apology* is new or provocative; instead, it completely typifies English Renaissance thought about literature.

AN APOLOGY FOR POETRY: RELIGION AND MORALITY

One assumption that Sidney makes is that all good things, including poetry, come from God. Humanity's purpose is to use those gifts to glorify God and also to promote morality. Christian beliefs pervaded Renaissance literature; people in the Renaissance were indoctrinated into Christian thinking in ways hard to imagine today, and most people were nominally—and some of them quite passionately—Christian. As will be seen below, major opponents of actors and theaters were often deeply devout Christians (many of them "Puritans") who strongly believed that plays and players were mostly instruments of the devil. And yet many other Renaissance Christians—including many of the most powerful—obviously approved of drama and other forms of "creative writing." How could they do so?

An Apology for Poetry provides many answers. At one point, for instance, Sidney (a very devout Christian and even, in some respects, a Puritan) argues that while nature can make individual virtuous people, poetry, by celebrating such people in vivid and powerful language, can make numerous people want to imitate such virtue. Or, as Sidney says in reference to an esteemed king of ancient Persia, great poets can "bestow a Cyrus upon the world to make many Cyruses." Sidney always assumes that the purpose of literature is to promote morality—an assumption enormously widespread in the Renaissance. People who attacked literature argued that it undermined virtue; people who defended it argued that it offered compelling moral lessons. At the very least, they argued that literature, as innocent recreation, did not *subvert* virtue.

If the poet, or "maker" (a common synonym), was able to create morally moving literature, who deserved the final credit? Sidney had a ready answer: We should "give right honor to the heavenly Maker of that maker, who, having made man to His own likeness, set him beyond and over all the works" of mere nature. "Which in nothing he [i.e., man] showeth so much as in poetry, when with the force of a divine breath he bringeth things forth surpassing her [i.e., nature's] doings." A great poem celebrating a virtuous person was in some ways even more important than the virtuous person him- or herself. A virtuous person might influence some contemporaries, but a great poem could inspire countless readers or audiences, in era after era, to want to imitate the virtue they read about or witnessed onstage. Similarly, evil examples powerfully set forth in well-written literature could help discourage evil behavior for generation after generation.

RELIGIOUS PRECEDENTS FOR POETRY

In one typical paragraph, Sidney sets forth a whole list of writers who, over the centuries, used literature to promote morality. Many did so by explicitly imitating

> the inconceivable excellencies of God. Such were David in his Psalms, Solomon in his Song of Songs, in his Ecclesiastes and Proverbs. Moses and Deborah, in their hymns, and the writer of Job, which [some scholars] do entitle the poetical part of Scripture: against these none will speak that hath the Holy Ghost in due holy reverence. In this kind, though in a full-wrong divinity, were Orpheus, Amphion, Homer in his hymns, and many other, both Greeks and Romans. And this poesy must be used by whosoever will follow Saint James's counsel in singing Psalms when they are merry, and I know is used with the fruit of comfort by some when, in sorrowful pangs of their death-bringing sins, they find consolation of the never-leaving goodness.

Later Sidney lists other writers who used poetry to impart philosophical and even scientific knowledge. All the best poets, he says, have used literature "both to delight and teach." In fact, they have themselves delighted "to move men to take that goodness in hand which, without delight, they would fly from as a stranger, and teach to make them know the goodness whereunto they are moved." In other words, the pleasure caused by poetry can make people not only embrace virtue but want to learn its true nature (which lies in knowledge of God).

Sidney believed that "the ending end"—that is, the ultimate purpose— "of all earthly learning [is] virtuous action." Philosophy taught the nature of right and wrong, and history provided specific examples of right and wrong behavior. But philosophy could strike most people as dry, abstract, and forbidding, while history dealt only with particular individuals. Only poetry, Sidney believed, could combine the specific with the abstract in ways that were genuinely pleasurable and ultimately *moving*. Literature could thus make people want to *be* virtuous. An especially rich passage sums up many of Sidney's arguments by asserting that the results of proper poetry are

> to teach goodness, and to delight the learners, since therein (namely in moral doctrine, the chief of all knowledges) [the poet] doth not only far pass the historian, but for instructing is well-nigh comparable to the philosopher, [and], for moving [i.e, for inspiring people to

actually *become* virtuous] leaveth him [i.e., the philosopher] behind him. Since the Holy Scripture, wherein there is no uncleanness, hath whole parts of it poetical, and that even our Savior, Christ, vouchsafed to use the flowers of it, since all his [i.e., the poet's] kinds are not only in their united forms, but in their severed dissections, fully commendable, I think (and think I think rightly) the laurel crown appointed for triumphant captains doth worthily of all other learnings honor the poet's triumph.

Poets, dramatists, and other creative writers in Renaissance England could not have asked for a better advocate than such a highly respected figure. Sidney defended poetry—in all its various genres—not only by celebrating it in his *Apology* but also by being a highly talented creative writer himself. He composed perhaps the first and most influential English novel or romance (*The Arcadia*), wrote a small but important drama or masque (*The Lady of May*), and, finally and perhaps most crucially, authored the most influential sonnet sequence of the period (*Astrophil and Stella*). Religious opponents of literature would always have to face the fact that one of the most devout and accomplished people in England had sanctioned literature not only in his treatise but also by his own example.

TO

THE MOST HIGH MIGHTIE AND MAGNIFICENT

E M P R E S S E

RENOWMED FOR PIETIE VERTVE AND ALL GRATIOVS GOVERNMENT

E L I Z A B E T H

BY THE GRACE OF GOD QVEENE OF ENGLAND

FRAVNCE AND IRELAND AND OF VIRGINIA

DEFENDOVR OF THE FAITH &c

HER MOST HVMBLE SERVAVNT

E D M V N D S P E N S E R

DOTH IN ALL HVMILITIE

DEDICATE PRESENT AND CONSECRATE

THESE HIS LABOVRS

TO LIVE WITH THE ETERNITIE OF HER FAME.

VOL. I.   * B

The dedication page of Edmund Spenser's *The Faerie Queen* as it appeared in a famous 1758 edition of the work.

VIRTUE IN RENAISSANCE LITERATURE

The key point on which both defenders of literature (such as Sidney) and opponents of literature could agree was that religious virtue was the most important trait of human life. Their main disagreement was whether literature in general and drama in particular promoted such virtue. Sidney believed that it could and did; the satirist Stephen Gosson, author of *Schoole of Abuse, containing a pleasant invective against Poets, Pipers, Plaiers, Jesters and such like Caterpillars of the Commonwealth* (1579), was far more skeptical. Proponents defended literature by arguing that it inspired moral behavior: It showed vivid examples of virtue and vice. They also praised literature for being well written and well crafted, but the ultimate purpose of excellent writing and craftsmanship was mainly moral.

A strong argument can be made that most English Renaissance literature does indeed teach, or try to teach, moral lessons. The works of such figures as Sidney, Edmund Spenser, Shakespeare, John Donne, and Ben Jonson, to name just a few, are all arguably moral in intent and—if read properly—in final effect. The same can be said of the prose of such writers as Thomas Nashe, Thomas Dekker, and the so-called "University Wits" (including John Lyly, Thomas Lodge, George Peele, and Robert Greene). Over the years, many scholars have offered numerous reasons to consider most of the "creative" writing produced during Shakespeare's era as fundamentally moral in emphasis, tone, and meaning.

Some scholars have argued that the supposed morality of Elizabethan litera-

Frontispiece of the 1635 publication of Donne's poems. The image, probably by printmaker William Marshall, is a portrait of Donne.

ture is not always evident and that some works by some writers—such as Marlowe and Donne—can be read as positively *immoral*. Certainly many Elizabethans would have agreed. Yet even works that *seem* immoral, such as much of the period's erotic poetry, can yield proper moral interpretations if they are read *ironically*, as, it can be argued, they were intended to be read. A classic case is John Donne's Elegy 19, "To His Mistress Going to Bed." This is one of the most sexually suggestive poems of the whole era, and it is easy to assume that Donne entirely sympathizes with the sexually aggressive male speaker. Yet the poem can also be read ironically, so that ultimately the speaker reveals himself as selfish, manipulative, exploitive, immoral, and irreligious. Another provocative poem by Donne—"The Flea"—may also undercut its cocky speaker. After all, at around the same time Donne was writing allegedly immoral erotic poems, he was also writing such deeply and profoundly religious verse as "Satire 3." Later he would even compose a whole series of "Holy Sonnets," as well as numerous other religious works, after becoming an Anglican priest.

Donne is just one intriguing case among many, and each case needs to be examined closely and carefully. Generally, however, it can almost always be argued that Renaissance works that may *seem* immoral and irreligious are simply teaching moral, religious lessons indirectly—through irony, parody, paradox, or some combination of these subversive devices. Renaissance writers knew that sometimes the most effective way to combat sin was not simply and openly to condemn it but rather to show it—as on a stage—and let people draw the obvious conclusions for themselves. Those people had, after all, been schooled since infancy about the Christian conclusions they were expected to draw. Many Renaissance writers seem to have trusted their audiences to deduce moral lessons without having them bluntly and blatantly spelled out. Sometimes, though, the irony was missed, as the following chapter will show. Some readers and audiences wanted to be preached at rather than being more subtly taught.

THE THEATER CHALLENGED AND DEFENDED

Most people today consider the dramas of Shakespeare's era among the greatest achievements of English culture. Opinion at the time, however, was far more divided. Many—including many highly educated and articulate writers and government officials—deeply regretted the rise of professional theaters in late sixteenth-century London. Public performances in London and elsewhere had, of course, existed for centuries, but they had had no settled, specifically designated venues. Instead, plays were often special (even annual) events. Players often moved from place to place, sometimes performing in the yards of inns, sometimes in town halls, sometimes in great houses, and sometimes on open-air carts in crowded urban squares. It was not until the late 1560s (about a decade after Elizabeth became queen and a few years after Shakespeare was born in 1564) that the first permanent theaters were constructed. London plays were now performed frequently in specially designed "playhouses," and the great age of English theater and of English *theaters* had begun. By the early 1590s, Shakespeare himself would be right in the thick of things, soon to establish an enviable reputation as a playwright.

ALLEY, FENTON, AND WHITE: EARLY ATTACKS ON THE THEATER

Responses to the growing prominence in London of plays, playhouses, and playwrights were often highly negative. Even before the first permanent theater was established, a writer named William Alley had in 1565 published condemnation of contemporary "jugglers, scoffers, jesters, [and] players." They could "say and do what they lust [i.e., wanted] be it never so fleshly and filthy" and could expect to be "heard with laughing and clapping of hands." Likewise, less than a decade later, Geoffrey Fenton also assailed players who "corrupt good moralities by wanton shows and plays." He urged that "they ought not to be suffered [i.e., allowed] to profane the Sabbath day in such sports, and much less to lose time on the days of travail [i.e., work]. All dissolute plays ought to be forbidden," although "comical and tragical shows of scholars in moral doctrines, and declamations in causes made to reprove and accuse vice and extol virtue, are very profitable." Right from the start, then, theater in Shakespeare's era was extremely controversial.

Fenton condemned the theater for offending God: "by wicked words, and blasphemy, impudent gestures, doubtful slanders, unchaste songs, and also by corruption of the wills of the players and the assistants." Such charges would be repeated continuously in later decades, and indeed three years later Thomas White was attacking "the common plays in London" and "the multitude that flocketh to them" in "sumptuous theater houses"— theaters that he considered "a continual monument of London's prodigality and folly." They were also, many believed, hotbeds of disease, especially the plague, an affliction often considered God's punishment for immorality. As White neatly put it, "the cause of plagues is sin, . . . and the cause[s] of sin are plays: therefore the cause of plagues are plays."

NORTHBROOK, GOSSON, AND MUNDAY: PLAYHOUSES AS CENTERS OF SIN

For many Elizabethans, playhouses were dens of iniquity. Thus John North-brook wrote in 1577 that "Satan hath not a more speedy way, and fitter school to work and teach his desire, to bring men and women into his snare of concupiscence and filthy lusts of wicked whoredom, than those places, and plays, and theaters are." According to Northbrook, many could "tarry at a vain play two of three hours, when as they [would] not abide scarce one hour at a sermon." He therefore advised readers that if they wanted to "learn how to be false and deceive your husbands, or husbands their wives, how to play the harlot, to obtain one's love, how to ravish, how to beguile, how to betray, to flatter, lie, swear, forswear, how to allure to whoredom, how to murder, how to poison, how to disobey and rebel against princes, to consume treasures prodigally, to move to lusts, to ransack and spoil cities and towns, to be idle, to blaspheme, to sing filthy songs of love, to speak filthily, to be proud, how to mock, scoff, and deride any nation," they could learn "at such interludes how to practice" such vices.

Obviously some of Northbrook's charges seem highly exaggerated, but they were hardly uncommon. In 1578 John Stockwood claimed that "a filthy play, with the blast of a trumpet," would "sooner call thither a thousand, than an hour's tolling of a bell" would "bring to the sermon a hundred." In the very next year, Stephen Gosson, an especially vocal critic of theater, asserted that "In our assemblies at plays in London, you shall see such heaving, and shoving, such itching and shouldering, to sit by the women; such care for their garments, that they be not trod on; such eyes to their laps, that no chips [of bread crust] light in them; such pillows to their backs, that they take no hurt; such masking in their ears, I know not what; such giving them pippins [i.e., apples] to pass the time; such playing at foot saunt [i.e., amorous toe touching] without cards; such ticking, such toying, such smiling, such winking, and such manning them [i.e., women] home when the sports are ended, that it is a right comedy to mark their behavior."

Gosson—at least in 1578—was not yet ready to condemn *all* plays and *all* actors, admitting that just "as some of the players are far from abuse, so some of their plays are without rebuke," including a few of his own. Moral plays were "good plays and sweet plays, and of all the plays the best plays and most to be liked," but in his opinion they were also very rare. Along with Gosson, Anthony Munday was another critic of plays who had written them and would later write many more. In 1580, however, he was ready to condemn "common plays" as "public enemies to virtue and religion: allurements unto sin; corrupters of good manners" and "mere brothel houses of bawdry" that were especially likely to corrupt married women and servants. Munday considered it shameful that powerful Elizabethan aristocrats often sponsored companies of actors and prevented London's magistrates from restraining players from practicing their craft.

GOSSON: PLAYHOUSES AS CHAPELS OF SATAN

Gosson considered the Elizabethan playhouse a "chapel of Satan" full "of young ruffians [and] harlots, utterly past all shame, who press to the forefront of the scaffolds [i.e., stage] . . . to show their impudency, and to be as an object to all men's eyes." Gosson realized (but greatly regretted) that powerful people at court delighted in plays and supported the players, but he especially condemned the theaters' supposed corruption of even (or especially) the players themselves. These included young boys prone to "wickedness," who were "trained up in filthy speeches" and "unnatural and unseemly gestures." Most actors were "roisters, brawlers, ill-dealers, boasters, lovers, loiterers, and ruffians," and the main purpose of playing was "to feed the world with sights, and fond [i.e., foolish] pastimes." Actors could "juggle in good earnest the money out of other men's purses into their own hands."

Gosson attacked again in 1582, noting that although the "abominable practices of plays in London" had "been by godly preachers . . . so zealously, so learnedly, so loudly cried out upon," the preachers' words had had little effect. Playing continued, and plays continued to have, according to Gosson, highly negative effects: "The beholding of troubles and miserable slaughters that are in tragedies drive us to immoderate sorrow, heaviness, womanish weeping and mourning, whereby we become lovers of dumps [i.e., melancholy or depression], and lamentation, both enemies to fortitude." Meanwhile, comedies "so tickle our senses with a pleasanter vein that they make us lovers of laughter and pleasure, without any mean [i.e., moderation], both foes to temperance." If anything good could be learned from plays, Gosson asserted, then the actors, who memorized dramas, should be the best people in the nation. Obviously, in Gosson's opinion, they were not.

Yet it wasn't merely their words that made plays dangerous. So did the theaters and the antics performed therein, for in addition to the "beauty of the houses and the stages," there was "garish apparel," as well as "masks, vaulting, tumbling, dancing of jigs, galliards, morrises [i.e., various kinds of dances], hobbyhorses," and juggling. Furthermore, plays inevitably violated proper standards of decorum and social rank. Shamefully, in stage plays it was common "for a boy to put on the attire, the gesture, the passions of a woman," since only boys played women in Elizabethan theaters. Likewise, on stage "a mean [i.e., common] person [could] take upon him the title of a prince with counterfeit port [i.e., deportment or behavior], and train [i.e., costuming]." Thus the actors "by outward signs . . . show themselves otherwise than they are," thus presenting "a lie." Both "tragedies and comedies," according to Gosson, "stir up affections [i.e., emotions], and affections are naturally planted in that part of the mind that is common to us with brute beasts." Plays, in other words, dehumanized people and made them behave like animals.

All this was clear, he thought, simply from observing the behavior of people in the theaters themselves: "In the playhouses at London, it is the fashion of youths to go first into the yard and to carry their eye through every gallery, then like unto ravens where they spy the carrion [i.e., dead flesh] thither thy fly, and press as near the fairest [women] as they can. . . . They give them pippins [i.e., apples], they dally with their garments to pass the time, they minister talk upon all occasions, and either bring them home to their houses on small acquaintance, or slip into taverns when the plays are done. He thinketh best of his painted sheath, and taketh himself for a jolly fellow, that is noted of most, to be busiest with women in all such places." Plays, then, not only depicted vice but encouraged it. It seemed a pity to people such as Gosson, including John Field in 1583, that "theaters should be full and churches be empty." This claim is probably a gross exaggeration. Yet the fact that such claims could be made—and made repeatedly—suggests that they contained at least an element of truth.

STUBBES AND SIDNEY: DRAMA ABUSED AND DEFENDED

Not everyone, of course, was willing to condemn plays completely. Some, such as Phillip Stubbes in 1583, claimed to censure merely *abuses* of drama. "For otherwise," he asserted, "(all abuses cut away) who seeth not that some kind of plays, tragedies and interludes, in their own nature are not only of great antientie [i.e., antiquity], but also very honest and very commendable exercises, being used and practiced in most Christian commonweals, [such] as [those] which contain matter . . . both of doctrine, erudition, good example, and wholesome instruction; and may be used, in time and place convenient, as conducible to example of life and reformation of manners. For such is our gross and dull nature [as humans], that what[ever] thing we see opposite before our eyes, do pierce further and print deeper in our hearts and minds, than that thing which is heard only with the ears." Stubbes believed, however, that numerous Elizabethan plays encouraged private vices and antisocial conduct. He considered actors "idle persons, doing nothing but playing and loitering, having their livings of the sweat of other men's brows."

Plays did, however, have their defenders, and one of the most important of these was none other than Sir Philip Sidney. In his *Apology for Poetry* (discussed in the previous section), Sidney argued that "comedy is an imitation of the common errors of our life," so "that the right use of comedy will (I think) by nobody be blamed, and much less of the high and excellent tragedy, that openeth the greatest wounds, and showeth forth the ulcers, that are covered with tissue; that maketh kings fear to be tyrants, and tyrants manifest their tyrannical humors; that with stirring the affects [i.e., emotions] of admiration and commiseration, teacheth the uncertainty of this world, and upon how weak foundations gilded roofs are builded." Sidney admitted, though, that

Habit of S. *Philip Sidney Kn.* *in 1580.*

An eighteenth century engraving of the writer and courtier Sir Philip Sidney.

few contemporary plays lived up to such standards. Indeed, he criticized the "gross absurdities" of many Elizabethan dramas, including how they were sometimes "neither right [i.e., proper] tragedies, nor right comedies, mingling kings and clowns" in a "mongrel tragi-comedy" and often provoking cheap laughs rather than genuine delight.

NASHE DEFENDS PLAYS, PLAYERS, AND PLAYWRIGHTS

By 1592, the feisty and always witty author Thomas Nashe was also defending plays. The fact that Shakespeare had by this point been living in London for several years and was already writing notable dramas makes Nashe's arguments all the more important. Nashe didn't simply defend plays in some ideal sense, as Sidney had; instead, he defended playgoing in contemporary London life, often for highly pragmatic reasons. He notes, for instance, that afternoon is a time when many men—such as courtiers, lawyers, law students, and soldiers—"do wholly bestow themselves upon pleasure," including "gaming [i.e., gambling], following of harlots, drinking, and seeing a play," and then he asks, "is it not then better . . . that they should betake them to . . . plays?" Better, in other words, to watch a play than to gamble, drink, or go whoring! Partly Nashe is joking, for he now argues that plays are not morally "extreme" but rather "a rare exercise in virtue." Sidney had claimed that Elizabethan dramas *might* potentially or occasionally be virtuous; Nashe asserts, on the other hand, that contemporary plays not only *could* teach but actually often *were* teaching valuable moral lessons and having positive ethical effects.

In phrasing that seems to allude at least in part to Shakespeare's early history plays, Nashe argues that the chief subjects of many contemporary dramas are "borrowed out of our English chronicles [i.e., books of history], wherein our forefathers' valiant acts . . . are revived, and they themselves raised from the grace of oblivion, and brought to plead their aged honors in open presence: than which, what can be a sharper reproof to these degenerate effeminate days of ours? How would it have joyed brave Talbot (the terror of the French) to think that after he had lyne [i.e., lain] two hundred years in his tomb, he should triumph again on the stage, and have his bones new embalmed with the tears of ten thousand spectators at least (at several times) who, in the tragedian [i.e., tragic actor] that represents his person, imagine they behold him fresh bleeding? . . . no immortality can be given a man on earth like unto plays."

Later, Nashe defends the social worth of drama even more emphatically: "In plays, all cozenages [i.e., tricks and deceptions], all cunning drifts over-gilded with outward holiness, all stratagems of war, all the cankerworms that breed on the rust of peace, are most lively anatomized; they [i.e., plays] show the ill success of treason, the fall of hasty climbers, the wretched end of usurpers, the misery of civil dissension, and how just God is evermore in punishing all murder." Nashe contends that although some people complain that plays draw young workers from their duties and into trouble, in fact plays keep them from trouble by giving them something better to do with their time. No play, Nashe proclaims, "encourageth any man to tumult or rebellion, but lays before such the halter [i.e., the prospect of being hanged in punishment] and the gallows." Similarly, he asserts that no play "praiseth or approveth pride, lust, whoredom, prodigality, or drunkenness, but beats them down utterly." The common charge that plays hinder trade results from the competitive jealousy of "vintners, alewives, and victualers [i.e., sellers of food], who surmise, [that] if there were no plays, they should have all the company that resort to them, lie bousing [i.e., drinking or boozing] and beer-bathing in their houses [i.e., taverns] every afternoon."

Responding to outraged moralists who disliked boys playing women, Nashe counters that "our players are not as the players beyond sea, a sort of squirting bawdy comedians, that have whores and common courtesans to play women's parts, and forebear no immodest speech or unchaste action that may procure laughter; but our scene is more stately furnished than ever it was in the time of Roscius [a great classical Roman actor], our representations honorable, and full of gallant resolution, not consisting, like theirs, of a pantaloon, a whore, and a zany [i.e., stereotypical comic characters], but of emperors, kings, and princes; whose true tragedies . . . they do vaunt." Perhaps no one before Nashe had defended actual Elizabethan theaters more vigorously or more wittily than he—partly, perhaps, because Nashe himself had actually written plays and may have had a major hand in Shakespeare's *Henry VI, Part One.*

CHETTLE AND CROSSE JOIN THE DEBATE

Yet another early defender of Elizabethan plays was Henry Chettle, also writing in 1592, in the early years of Shakespeare's career as a dramatist. Replying to the standard charge that plays promoted vice, Chettle answered with the equally standard assertion that from the very same "flower the Bee and Spider suck honey" (on the one hand) "and poison" (on the other). What mattered, then, were the audience's motives and disposition rather than the play's phrasing. Anyone seeking ethical profit from plays could find it; anyone seeking cheap pleasure could find that, too. "In plays it fares as in books," Chettle argued; "vice cannot be reproved except it be discovered [i.e., depicted]." Theater could only rebuke bad behavior by first actually showing it on stage. Players should not be faulted if audiences imitated the misconduct the players depicted and intended to rebuke. There was nothing wrong, Chettle believed, with mirth "in seasonable [i.e., appropriate] time," and if disturbances sometimes broke out in theaters, that was not the fault of most members of the audience but rather of "some lewd mates that long for innovation." Such "mates" used any disturbances as chances for thefts.

Yet despite the best efforts of drama's defenders, many observers remained unconvinced of the value of plays. Thus Henry Crosse in 1603 (the year Queen Elizabeth died and King James succeeded her) argued that "these modern plays, wherewith the world is now so pestered, are altogether made upon lascivious arguments, and serve as the very organs and instruments to vanity." In them, he claimed, "the honor due to God, and reverence to man, is laid aside, virtue disrobed, and vice exalted; and instead of morality, fictions, lies, and scurrilous matter is foisted in, and is cunningly conveyed into the hearts of the assistants, whereby they are transformed into what they see acted before them: for the rustic and common sort are apes, that will imitate in themselves that which they see done by others. Or if they [i.e., playwrights] stuff their scene with one good precept, or well-worded instruction, what power hath that to move to virtue? . . . it is immediately profaned with their exorbitant foolery, as pure water in a foul and muddy cistern."

PATRONS OF PLAYS: FROM THE GREAT TO THE LOWLY

By the time Crosse wrote, perhaps the most famous playwright in London was Shakespeare, who had already written many of his most famous plays, including *Romeo and Juliet*, *A Midsummer Night's Dream*, *Julius Caesar*, *As You Like It*, and *Hamlet*, among many others. One sometimes wonders which plays people like Crosse were attending! Obviously, however, not everyone agreed with the critics' harsh assessments. Important nobles had long patronized dramatists and theater companies, even making them official servants. Indeed, the new monarch no sooner arrived in London than he renamed Shakespeare's company The King's Men, taking them officially under his wing. Other royals followed suit, with the queen and crown prince both sponsoring acting companies. Although attacks on plays, players, and playwrights were common, the theater survived and flourished thanks to the interest and support of successive monarchs and other prominent aristocrats. Players often performed at the royal court, and indeed a common justification for allowing actors and theaters to exist was the argument that the court needed entertainment, and actors needed places to rehearse.

Critics such as Crosse sometimes objected less to the plays themselves than to some of the people the theater attracted. This much is clear from Crosse's already-quoted reference to "the rustic and common sort," but he elaborates later by referring to the audience as "the ignorant" and by asking, "What true glory then can they [i.e., players] justly merit, that are praised by the witless and brainsick multitude?" According to Crosse and others, the "common haunters" of theaters were, "for the most part, the lewdest persons in the land, apt for pilfery, perjury, forgery, or any roguery; the very scum, rascality, and baggage of the people; thieves, cut-purses, shifters, cozeners; briefly, an unclean generation, and spawn of vipers." As this long list suggests, Crosse was hardly objective. Elizabethan audiences were far more diverse and complex than he implies. But Crosse's rhetoric was typical. Many opponents of theater—like Crosse himself—apparently envied the money that could be earned by writing plays and acting in them. Thus Crosse mocks "these copper-lace gentlemen [who] grow rich" and are "puffed up in such pride and self-love as they envy their equals, and scorn their inferiors."

Besides making some actors and dramatists rich, plays also, in Crosse's opinion, resulted in numerous other social ills. Thus "many poor, pinched, needy creatures, that live [off] alms, and that have scarce neither cloth to their back, nor food for the belly, yet will make hard shift but they will see a play, let wife and children beg, languish in penury, and all they can rap and rend is little enough to lay upon such vanity." Poor people, Crosse thought, were spending their meager funds on playgoing rather than on necessities. Yet plays were just the tip of the iceberg; it would be better, Crosse believed, "that all love-books, sonnets, and vile pamphlets were burned, and no more suffered to be printed, nor filthy plays rehearsed, which are bellows to blow the coals of lust, soften the mind, and make it flexible to evil inclination." Literature should be permitted only after being "first seen and allowed, by some of approved and discreet judgment."

JONSON'S MISGIVINGS

Even some leading dramatists were troubled by various plays. Ben Jonson, Shakespeare's friend and rival, asked what "learned or liberal [i.e., free] soul" did not already "abhor" the "present trade of the stage in all their miscellaneous interludes." The stage, Jonson claimed, was often a place where "nothing but the garbage of the time is uttered, and that with such impropriety of phrase, such plenty of solecisms [mistakes in speaking or writing], such dearth of sense, so bold prolepses [anachronisms], so racked metaphors, [along] with brothelry able to violate the ear of a pagan, and blasphemy to turn the blood of a Christian to water." Jonson, unlike other critics, was at least as troubled by the allegedly poor artistry of many plays as by their supposed immorality. He felt that his own "fame, and the reputations of diverse honest and learned" writers were "in question, when a name [i.e., that of "poet"] so full of authority, antiquity, and all great mark" had become, through the "insolence" of some, "the lowest scorn of the age." He considered it shameful that poets were now "subject to the petulance of every vernaculous orator," especially since poets had once been "the care of kings." Indeed, he claimed that he wrote *Volpone* partly "to put the snaffle [i.e., bit] in their mouths that cry out [that] we never punish vice in our interludes."

HEYWOOD'S DEFENSE OF ACTORS AND ACTING

It was only in 1612, near the end of Shakespeare's career, that a player and playwright, Thomas Heywood, explicitly defended acting. Heywood argued in his *An Apology for Actors* that a mere spoken or written "description is only a shadow received by the ear, but not perceived by the eye." Likewise, "lively portraiture is merely a form seen by the eye, but can neither show action, passion, motion, or any other gesture, to move the spirits of the beholder to admiration." At plays, however, it appears "as if the personator were the man personated: so bewitching a thing is lively and well spirited action, that it hath power to new mold the hearts of the spectators and fashion them to the shape of any noble and notable attempt." Replying to religious critics of drama, Heywood noted that neither Christ nor any apostle had ever condemned the theater, even though theaters were common during their times. Indeed, Heywood argued that drama had never once been censured in either the Old or New Testaments, thus suggesting that religious critics were overscrupulous zealots.

Theater, Heywood maintained, could be merely one of many "moderate recreations" ordained by God for man's use, and theaters were especially appropriate in large capitals such as London. The ancient Greeks and Romans had embraced theaters and plays, and contemporary colleges and universities also sanctioned plays and acting. England had, in the past several decades, produced numerous actors who deserved to enjoy lasting reputations. They had long been applauded not only by Elizabeth herself but also

"Volpone Adoring His Treasures." Illustration by Aubrey Beardsley for an 1898 edition of Ben Jonson's *Volpone*.

by broad audiences in general. Inevitably, of course, some actors fell short of the ideal not only in their abilities to perform but also in their licentious personal lives, and indeed Heywood urged that since actors were "men that stand in the broad eye of the world, so should our manners, gestures, and behaviors savor of such government and modesty to deserve the good thoughts and reports of all men, and to abide the sharpest censures." Yet he also noted that many actors were already men "of substance, of government, of sober lives, and temperate carriages, house-keepers [i.e., home owners], and contributory to all duties enjoined them, equally with them that are ranked with the most bountiful." If a few actors failed to live exemplary lives, the majority should not be censured "for the misdeeds of some."

According to Heywood, theater was not only ancient and dignified but was "even in these days by the best [people], without exception, favorably tolerated." Thus it was not simply commoners who would pay money to see plays; many of the most highly educated and socially prominent would as well, and they approved of what they saw. Theater in Shakespeare's London could not have survived without the sanction of the powerful, including the monarch, leading aristocrats, the royal court, and much of the rest of the contemporary power structure. Commoners may have paid pennies to crowd into theaters, but those theaters could never have opened—or remained open—without the permission of leading authorities. Theater, according to Heywood, was "an ornament" to London, "which strangers of all nations, repairing hither, report of in their countries, beholding them here with some admiration: for what variety of entertainment can there be in any city in Christendom, more than in London?"

HEYWOOD ON THEATER'S IMPACT ON LANGUAGE AND ON SOCIETY

Heywood also defended theater, however, in far more interesting ways. He argued that English itself was, thanks to the theater, "continually refined, every writer striving in himself to add a new flourish unto it; so that in process, from the most rude and unpolished tongue, it is grown to a most perfect and composed language, and many excellent works and elaborate poems writ in the same, [so] that many nations grow enamored of our tongue ([which was] before despised)." Thanks to theater's impact, English had become far richer than it had been even 60 years earlier; it was now something of which all English people could be proud.

In addition, Heywood maintained, "plays have made the ignorant more apprehensive [i.e., perceptive], taught the unlearned the knowledge of many famous histories, [and] instructed such as cannot read in the discovery of all our English chronicles." Plays were written "with this aim and carried with this method, to teach the subjects obedience to their king; to show the people the untimely ends of such as have moved tumults [i.e., caused political disturbances], commotions, and insurrections; and to present them with [the] flourishing estate of such as live in obedience, exhorting them to allegiance, [and] dehorting them from all traitorous and felonious stratagems." Of course, plays were probably not nearly as uniformly conservative as Heywood suggests, but he is hardly the only contemporary defender of drama to make these kinds of claims.

HEYWOOD ON THE MORALITY OF DRAMA

The main purpose of contemporary theater, according to Heywood, was to promote morality. "If we present a foreign history, the subject is so intended that, in the lives of the Romans, Grecians, or others, either the virtues of our country-men are extolled, or their vices reproved." This era's drama sought, or so he claimed, "to persuade men to humanity and good life, to instruct them in civility and good manners, showing them the fruits of honesty, and the end of villainy." Comedy was "pleasantly contrived with merry accidents, and intermixed with apt and witty jests," thereby providing "harmless mirth." Yet comedy also presented "slovenly and unhandsome behavior" so that audiences might "reform that simplicity in themselves, which others make their sport, lest they happen to become the like subject of general scorn."

Especially interesting is Heywood's assertion that romantic comedies were intended to deride "foolish inamorates [i.e., lovers] who spend their ages, their spirits, nay themselves, in the servile and ridiculous employments of their mistresses." Comedies were also "mingled with sportful accidents, [in order] to recreate" people who were "wholly devoted to melancholy, which corrupts the blood: or to refresh such weary spirits as are tired with labor, or study" and "to moderate the cares and heaviness of the mind," so that people "may return to their trades and faculties with more zeal and earnestness, after some small[,] soft and pleasant retirement." Comedies also taught many useful lessons. Sometimes they depicted "courtesans," in order to "divulge their subtleties and snares, in which young men may be entangled," thereby showing such youths how to avoid being duped. Pastoral comedies, meanwhile, showed "the harmless love of shepherds diversely moralized, distinguishing betwixt the craft [i.e., deceit] of the city, and the innocence of the sheep-cote."

In short, Heywood claimed that "there is neither tragedy, history, comedy, moral, or pastoral, from which an infinite use cannot be gathered." Yet he carefully noted that he did *not* speak "in the defense of any lascivious shows, scurrilous jests, or scandalous invectives; if there be any such, I banish them quite from my patronage." He specifically endorsed Sidney's views, paraphrasing him as having asserted that "Tragedies well handled be a most worthy kind of poesy" and that "Comedies make men see and shame at their faults." According to Heywood himself, contemporary plays presented people "with the ugliness of their vices, to make them the more abhor them." Thus he claimed that "drunkards" were "naturally [i.e., realistically] imitated in our plays, to the applause of the actor, content of the auditory [i.e., satisfaction of the audience], and reproving of the vice."

Yet drunkenness was not the only vice depicted. "Art thou addicted to prodigality? envy? cruelty? perjury? flattery? or rage?" If so, then "Our scenes afford thee store of [i.e., many] men to shape your lives by, who be frugal, loving, gentle, trusty, without soothing [i.e., flattery], and in all things temperate. Wouldst thou be honorable? Just, friendly, moderate, devout, merciful, and loving concord? Thou mayest see [in plays] many of their fates and ruins who have been dishonorable, unjust, false, gluttonous, sacrilegious, bloody-minded, and broachers of dissention." Heywood even recounted a famous story (also reported by various other defenders of drama) in which a play had supposedly helped uncover a murder.

According to Heywood, as this play—featuring the ghost of a husband murdered by his wife—was acted, "a townswoman (till then of good estimation and report) finding her conscience (at this presentment) extremely troubled, suddenly screeched and cried out Oh my husband, my husband! I see the ghost of my husband fiercely threatening and menacing me." She thereupon confessed to having murdered him, and so a crime was solved thanks to contemporary drama. As if one such story were insufficient, Heywood related several more, including one in which a woman, after watching a play featuring a man who died after having a nail driven through his skull, admitted the murder of her own husband, 12 years earlier, in precisely that manner. "This being publically confessed," Heywood concluded, "she was arraigned, condemned, adjudged, and burned."

By this point, Heywood's defense of contemporary plays was almost finished. All that was left was to note how many emperors and monarchs, throughout history, had permitted and indeed even patronized drama, including "the thrice virtuous virgin, Queen Elizabeth," as well as her sister, brother, and father, and also her successor, King James. Heywood rejected any recent drama guilty of "inveighing against the state, the court, the law, the city, and their governments, with the particularizing [through personal satire] of private men's humors (yet alive), noble-men and others." Such satire was especially offensive when mouthed by child actors, as in fact it often was. Heywood hoped that no one would blame adult actors for such conduct, since, he claimed, they had "ever been careful and provident to shun the like." Whether this was entirely true, of course, was a matter of definite dispute.

"JOHN GREENE" DISPUTES THOMAS HEYWOOD

Heywood was answered at length in 1615 in *A Refutation of the Apology for Actors*, attributed only to "I. G.," commonly identified as John Greene. Greene began by noting that although "Plays have ever been condemned by godly Christians, . . . now the impiety of players is grown to such excess that they take upon themselves to defend their quality." God, wrote Greene, had never allowed drama to flourish among the ancient Hebrews. To make matters worse, plays, in his opinion, were "full of idle and vain words," which Christ had condemned, and they were also full of "obscene speeches, which Saint Paul forbids," just as Paul had also forbidden "lies and profane fables." Greene also believed that plays were brimming with "all obscenity, acts of fornication, and practices of strumpets and cozeners [i.e., cheaters], and full of scurrility, fooleries, mocks [i.e., satire] and mows [i.e., derisive grimaces], spoken against by Saint Paul." In addition, they showcased "railing, reviling, backbiting, quipping, taunts, and evil speaking, which is forbidden in the ninth commandment." Religious objections to drama were common during the English Renaissance, but defenders of plays often defended them precisely by claiming that they were morally and theologically wholesome.

JOHN GREENE ON A FEW REASONS TO DISLIKE PLAYS

Greene, however, was not convinced. He argued that "The matter of tragedies is haughtiness, arrogancy, ambition, pride, injury, anger, wrath, envy, hatred, contention, war, murder, cruelty, rapine, incest, rovings, depredations, piracies, spoils, robberies, rebellions, treasons, killing, hewing, stabbing, dagger-drawing, fighting, butchery, treachery, villainy, etc., and all kinds of heroic evils whatsoever. Of comedies the matter is love, lust, lechery, bawdry, scortation [i.e., fornication], adultery, uncleanness, pollution, wantonness, chambering [i.e., sexual indulgence], courting, jesting, mocking, flouting, foolery, venery, drabbery [i.e., harlotry], knavery, cozenage, cheating, hypocrisy, flattery, and the like. And as complements and appendants to both kinds of plays is swearing, cursing, oaths, and blasphemies, etc."

Greene, with his wonderful talent for making lists, adds several more similar compilations. In response to anyone who might argue that plays reprehended the vices they depicted, he answered that "players assume an unlawful office to themselves of instruction and correction: and therefore it becometh sin unto them, because God never ordained them unto it, which is the reason that never any profited in goodness but in wickedness by them." Thus Greene felt that dramatists usurped the roles both of ministers and of civil authorities: "for our lives ought not to be the subjects for poets to play upon, but for lawful magistracy, and thoroughly informed justice to judge upon." Plays nourished vice, encouraged idleness, and drew people away from churches: "For you shall have them [i.e., people] flock thick and three-fold to the play-houses, and with all celerity make speed to enter in them, lest they should not get place near enough unto the stage (so prone and ready are they to do evil) when the temple of God shall remain bare and empty."

Who visited theaters? According to Greene, typical playgoers included "the profane gallant to feed his pleasure; the city dames to laugh at their own shames; the country clown [i.e., hick] to tell wonders when he comes home of the vanities he hath seen; the bawds [i.e., sexual panderers] to entice; the whores and courtesans to set themselves to sale; the cutpurse to steal; the pickpocket to filch; the knave to be instructed in more cozening tricks; youth to learn amorous conceits; some for one wicked purpose, some for another, none to any good intent, but all fruitlessly to misspend their time. But among any others that go to the theaters, when shall you see an ancient citizen, a chaste matron, a modest maid, a grave senator, a wise magistrate, a just judge, a godly preacher, a religious man not blinded in ignorance, but making conscience of his ways? You shall never see any of these men at plays, for they count it shameful and ignominious, even an act of reproach that may redound unto them." Plays, he continues, are demonic. The "theater is Satan's synagogue and the devil's own house."

Greene's tract was published in 1615, the year before Shakespeare died, but arguments about theater continued for many years. Drama in Shakespeare's day was by no means as widely respected then as now. Many people obviously valued it, but many others just as clearly saw it as a figurative plague on England—a plague that might eventually lead to even greater punishment from God.

OFFICIAL RESPONSES TO THE THEATER: 1559

Actual—rather than figurative—plague genuinely concerned government officials when they thought about London's theaters. In the playhouses, numerous people gathered during the hot summer months, when plague was often rampant. The theaters were frequently closed by government edict during times of mass infection, but many Londoners, including many important citizens, wished the playhouses could be closed permanently—and for all kinds of reasons. Hostility toward drama in London began early and lasted for many years. Efforts to control, if not entirely ban, the theater are well documented.

In May 1559, for instance, in the second year of Queen Elizabeth's reign, a proclamation forbade performances of interludes except at officially approved times of the year. "The Queen's Majesty," it declared, "doth straightly [i.e., immediately] forbid all manner [of] Interludes to be played either openly or privately, except the same be notified beforehand, and licensed within any city or town . . . by the Mayor and other chief officers." Similar regulations were imposed throughout the country, making this proclamation one of the earliest—but certainly not the last—attempt by Elizabethan governments to control drama.

The same proclamation also declared that government officers should "permit [no dramas] to be played wherein either matters of religion or of the governance of the [state] shall be handled or treated, . . . nor to be handled before any audience, but of grave and discreet persons." Violations might lead to arrest and imprisonment. Of course, efforts at control did not mean that control was successfully achieved, but this early proclamation reveals the concerns and motives that would preoccupy the government for years to come. Religious and political topics were especially touchy issues. Many people believed that holy matters should not be profaned by being dealt with onstage. These were years of enormous religious tension and outright conflict between Catholics and Protestants, with the queen, a Protestant, trying to find a viable "middle way." It was impossible anywhere in Europe to completely separate politics from religion: The two were complexly intertwined. Faith was never really a private matter: The government always had some interest in it.

The government was concerned, in fact, not only with plays performed but also with plays printed. Many kinds of publications had to be preapproved, according to a decree issued in June 1559: "And because many pamphlets, plays and ballads be oftentimes printed, wherein regard would be had, that nothing therein should be either heretical, seditious, or unseemly for Christian ears: her majesty likewise commandeth, that no manner of person shall enterprise to print any such, except the same be to him licensed by such of her majesty's Commissioners, or three of them." These men would ensure that such printed matter would conform to recent statutes "tending [toward] uniformity of order in Religion." Plays needed supervision, not

"Rainbow" portrait of Elizabeth I, ca. 1600–1602. *(Attributed to Isaac Oliver and Marcus Gheeraerts)*

only before they were performed but also if they happened to be printed. If not, the commonwealth might become infected with dangerous ideas.

OFFICIAL OBJECTIONS TO PLAYS: 1569–74

Disease continued to preoccupy the authorities. A decree from May 1569 by the City of London noted that many people gathered frequently "to hear and see certain stage plays, interludes, and other disguisings, on the Sabbath days and other solemn feasts." They were typically "close pestered together in small rooms." These were unhealthy environments, "especially during this time of summer," when diseases were common. Therefore, "great infection with the plague, or some other infectious diseases," might "rise and grow," afflicting not only Londoners but also visitors, who would take their diseases back home with them. Because of such concerns, play performances were often banned for weeks or months. Worries about plague and about theaters as sites of transmission occur repeatedly in official documents.

Civic authorities also associated theaters with many other problems, including all kinds of inappropriate conduct. Thus a London decree dated December 1574 noted that "sundry great disorders and inconveniences have been found to ensue to the City by the inordinate haunting of great multitudes of people, especially youth, to plays, interludes, and shows." These had been the "occasion of frays and quarrels, evil practices of incontinency in great inns [where plays were sometimes staged], having chambers and secret places adjoining to their open stages and galleries, inveigling and alluring of maids, especially orphans and good citizens' children under age, to privy and unmeet [i.e., unfit] contracts, [and] the publishing of unchaste, uncomely and unshamefast speeches and doings."

This, however, was just the beginning. Plays were also accused of "withdrawing of the Queen's Majesty's Subjects from divine service on Sundays and holy days." Additional offenses included providing occasions for the "unthrifty waste of money of the poor and fond [i.e., foolish] persons, sundry robberies by picking and cutting of purses, uttering of popular, busy, and seditious matters, and many other corruptions of youth and other enormities, besides that also sundry slaughters and mayhemings [sic] of the Queen's subjects have happened by ruins [i.e., the collapse] of scaffolds, frames, and stages, and by engines [i.e. machines], weapons, and [gun]powder used in plays." Numerous documents make the same allegations. Plays, for many civic authorities, were prime sources of social sickness. Little wonder, then, that efforts to control or suppress them went on for decades.

FRICTIONS BETWEEN LONDON AUTHORITIES AND THE ROYAL PRIVY COUNCIL: 1581–82

Ostensibly, many performances in London were merely rehearsals so that the players, especially if sponsored by aristocrats, could do adequate jobs when called to perform before the queen. In the early years of professional theater in London, the players were often poor and needed their jobs as actors to support their families. The authorities sometimes allowed them to perform (when performances had otherwise been temporarily banned) for precisely this reason. Thus in December 1581, once the plague had mainly passed, the royal Privy Council granted a petition from some players "humbly desiring that as well in respect of their poor estates, having no other means to sustain them, their wives and their children but by their exercise of playing," and because they had only been "brought up from their youth in the practice and profession of music and playing," they should be allowed to perform again. In general, the Privy Council and royal court were far more tolerant of players and playing than were the London authorities. This is hardly surprising: Players were often the liveried servants of powerful people, including the queen and other aristocrats.

Evidence of the hostility of London authorities toward the players abounds. In April 1582, for instance, the lord mayor forbade, upon pain of punishment, attendance at plays by any members of local guilds (i.e., professional societies), as well as any of their servants, apprentices, journeymen, or children. Such injunctions, however, were obviously never completely effective: Playgoing continued, with occasional interruptions, until the theaters were finally closed by civil war in 1642, not to reopen until 1660. No sooner had the lord mayor issued his 1582 injunction than the royal Privy Council countermanded it, ordering him to suppress only plays that bred "corruption of manners and conversation among the people" but instructing him to permit plays that seemed "fit to yield honest recreation and no example of evil." Such conflicting commands—with city officials opposed by royal officers—continued for years.

TENSIONS CONTINUE: 1584

Sometimes the actors themselves became involved in the dispute. Thus, in late 1584 the queen's own players petitioned the Privy Council, asking to be allowed to perform within the precincts of London so they would be properly prepared to play before the queen. London authorities quickly responded, telling the royal councilors that the "lewd matters of plays [had] increased" and claiming that "in the haunt unto them were found many dangers, both for religion, state, honesty of manners, unthriftiness of the poor, and danger of infection." The city authorities advised that the players should be allowed to perform only in private houses, since any playing "in the throng of a multitude" risked exposing the queen herself to the plague. In response to the players' claims that they needed to perform to make their livings, the city authorities objected to the very professionalization of actors. They reminded the Privy Council that in former times players were simply amateurs who did not expect to survive by playing alone.

The London authorities, writing to the Privy Council, also noted "how uncomely" it seemed "for youth to run straight from prayer to plays, from God's service to the Devil's." Any toleration of the queen's own players, they cautioned, would lead to playing by others. London authorities *were* willing to allow some playing "in private houses, at weddings etc. without public assemblies." They were also willing to permit open performances as long as they did not take place until plague deaths had fallen, for 20 days, to below 50 per week. They wanted no plays performed on the Sabbath, nor any playing on other holy days until after evening prayer, nor any people allowed into audiences until after such prayer. They wanted no playing to take place during the dark, and they wanted all audience members back in their homes before dark. Only the queen's own players should be tolerated, not any others.

A SOLDIER COMPLAINS (1587)

Even the royal authorities occasionally restricted players and publications. Besides often sensibly banning performances during times of plague, they declared, in 1586, that all books, including playbooks, should be approved by a royal censor before being printed. Nevertheless, courtiers were themselves sometimes criticized for being too tolerant of plays and players. Thus one anonymous letter writer, who identified himself as a soldier, complained in 1587 to one of the queen's councilors that the "daily abuse of stage plays is such an offense to the godly, and so great a hindrance to the gospel" that "the papists [i.e., Catholics] do exceeding rejoice." Playing, in other words, cast Protestants (including the queen and her councilors, whose names were often mentioned in public advertisements for plays) in a highly unflattering light.

According to this letter writer, no sooner did bells summon people to church than trumpets called them to theaters, "whereat the wicked faction of Rome laugheth for joy, while the godly weep for sorrow. Woe is me!" He continued, "the play houses are pestered [i.e., full of people], when churches are naked; at the one it is not possible to get a place, at the other void [i.e., empty] seats are plenty." Fortunately, God had graciously restrained himself from punishing such sin. Yet the writer considered it "a woeful sight to see two hundred proud players jet [i.e., strut or swagger] in the silks, where five hundred poor people starve in the streets." If theaters continued to operate, they should at least pay weekly pensions to the poor—an idea also advocated by many others.

FURTHER COMPLAINTS AND MORE CONTROLS: 1589

London's lord mayor sent an especially interesting letter in 1589 to Queen Elizabeth's chief adviser. By this time Shakespeare's playwriting career was already under way, and so it is interesting to read how defiant some players could be in their dealings with authority. The mayor complained that he had called before him two companies of actors, sponsored by prominent aristocrats, and had commanded them to temporarily cease performing. One company "very dutifully obeyed," but the other "played that afternoon, to the great offense of the better sort that knew they were prohibited." The mayor, therefore, committed some of the players to jail.

The Privy Council itself, in 1589, decided that all plays should be approved by royal censors before being acted, let alone published, particularly since the players were handling, "without judgment or decorum . . . matters of divinity and state." Actors would now be expected to deliver their plays to royal officials before performances, and the officials would "strike out or reform such parts and matters as they shall find unfit and undecent." This task belonged mainly to the "master of the revels," who earned a fee each time he perused a play. It was in his interests, then, not to oppose plays altogether, just as it was in the interests of the players and playwrights to submit nothing that might seem too provocative. The relationship between the master and the players could be mutually profitable if it were sensibly maintained.

THE 1590S: FURTHER DISPUTES AS SHAKESPEARE'S CAREER DEVELOPS

By the early 1590s, when Shakespeare was beginning to write some particularly important works (such as *Richard III*), playhouses had become so prominent in London that other businesses—including inns, taverns, and places to eat—benefitted from their presence. In 1592, Lord Strange's Men petitioned the Privy Council for the reopening of their playhouse, across the Thames River from London, arguing that keeping it closed was a "great hindrance" to the watermen who rowed passengers from one riverbank to the other. The watermen themselves also soon petitioned, claiming that they had had "much help and relief for us [and] our poor wives and children by means of the resort of such people as come unto the said playhouse." Both petitions succeeded, although by January 1593 the Privy Council was again ordering the theaters closed for fear of plague. Such closings and reopenings had become part of the rhythm of London life, with the city's authorities pleased by closings and the royal Privy Council more permissive.

In 1594, for example, the lord mayor, hearing of plans for a new theater across the Thames, asked the royal government "rather to suppress all such places built for that kind of exercise" than to allow erec-

A nineteenth-century engraving of William Shakespeare by Benjamin Holl.

tion of "any more of the same sort." The mayor, in an especially intriguing passage, said he knew that some people defended plays by claiming that "the people must have some kind of recreation, and that policy requireth to divert idle heads and other ill-disposed [people] from other worse practice by this kind of exercise." Plays, in other words, helped prevent real trouble-making, at least according to some.

But the mayor remained unconvinced. He urged the queen's chief minister to "observe the fruits and effects" of plays: They contained "nothing else but unchaste fables, lascivious devices, shifts [i.e., acts] of cozenage, and matters of like sort." Most people who attended plays, he said, were "the base and refuse sort of people or such young gentlemen as have small regard of credit [i.e., reputation] or conscience." Such people copied the vices they saw in plays, and the playhouses themselves had become the "ordinary places of meeting for all vagrant persons and masterless men that hang about the city," not to mention "thieves, horse-stealers, whoremongers, cozeners, cony-catching persons [i.e shysters], practicers of treason," and similar sorts of people. Their activities displeased God and hurt good citizens. At the theaters, serving men learned how to cheat their masters, and in general the whole population learned many other bad habits. This, at least, is what the mayor claimed, and there is little doubt that the playhouses often did attract unsavory people and unwholesome behavior.

Similar complaints were lodged two years later by another mayor and other aldermen. Indeed, the more one reads these objections, the more one notices their similarities. Since such complaints were continual, few problems associated with the theaters seem to have ever been really "solved," at least in the eyes of civic authorities. Complaints from one

PURITANISM

The "Puritans" were a broad and often internally divided group of Protestants who wished to purify the English church of Catholic traditions even more than it had been purified already during the Protestant Reformation. The term *Puritan* was originally used as a term of abuse by people unsympathetic to such changes, and many historians have even doubted the current usefulness of the term. Indeed, some historians argue that the so-called Puritans differed little from their opponents in basic theological assumptions and that the importance of theological disputes within the Anglican church has often been exaggerated. Nevertheless, differences of opinion did exist, and they became increasingly significant between the 1580s and the 1630s and helped contribute, eventually, to the outbreak of civil war in the 1640s.

Puritans tended to emphasize the importance of sermons rather than external ceremonies: They stressed genuinely knowing the word of God (including knowledge of the Bible) rather than merely adhering to outward religious observances. They tended to be stricter in their ideas about the kinds of behavior God permitted than their opponents were. They were more likely, for instance, to believe that Sundays should be mainly devoted to worship and religious study, rather than given over to relaxation, sports, or other pleasant pastimes. Puritans emphasized, even more than most Protestants, the ideal of an individual's personal relationship with God, and they grew increasingly distrustful of the kind of church government that emphasized the power of bishops. They saw themselves as an especially "godly" group of believers who took their religion quite seriously, while their opponents increasingly saw them as intolerant, inflexible, somewhat grim, and even hypocritical. Puritans were often perceived as radical Protestants in the same way that Jesuits were often perceived as radical Catholics. Queen Elizabeth and King James found both groups to be the source of much difficulty during their reigns, as both monarchs tended to favor a more conservative or moderate form of Protestant faith and worship.

"Marry, sir, sometimes he is a kind of puritan."
—*Twelfth Night* (2.3.138)

decade usually strongly resembled complaints from another, although sometimes an especially vivid detail was tossed into the mix. Thus, in July 1597 the mayor and aldermen noted that many theatergoers who had open "sores" but who were not yet "heart-sick" often took "occasion to walk abroad and recreate themselves by hearing a play," thus putting thousands at risk of catching the plague. No wonder the authorities were often exasperated! Sometimes members of the Privy Council adopted a hard line against playhouses and players; in general, though, they were far more lenient than the mayors and aldermen of London wanted them to be.

DEFENSES OF THEATER BY THE PLAYWRIGHTS

The theatrical world that Shakespeare entered, then, created enormous controversy, especially during the first half of his career. One might have expected him and his fellow dramatists to respond to these disputes. Sometimes they did, but certainly not to any great degree. Only Thomas Heywood, in the treatise already discussed, penned a lengthy, free-standing defense of actors and of acting, and this was published when the career of the era's greatest dramatist was almost over. Other dramatists defended their profession in passing, usually in prologues or epilogues or in comments by theatrical characters themselves.

In Thomas Middleton's 1596 *The Mayor of Quinborough,* for instance, a Puritan opponent of the theater is mocked by being forced to watch a play, to which he responds, "O tyranny, tyranny! revenge it, tribulation! / For rebels there are many deaths; but sure the only way / To execute a puritan, is seeing of a play." Obviously Middleton was mocking hyper-religious critics of the playhouses. In fact, mockery of Puritans was quite common in plays, for this reason and for others. Indeed, in *The Revenge of Bussy d'Ambois* (1606), George Chapman has a character spend many lines defending plays from Puritan attacks. Plays, he says, often profitably call attention to social vices and abuses, and "The stage and actors are not so contemptful [i.e., worthy of contempt] / As any innovating puritan, / And ignorant sweater-out of zealous envy, / Would have the world imagine." Dedicating the 1612 printing of his play *The Widow's Tears,* Chapman more positively defends drama, noting that in foreign countries plays were patronized by dukes and princes. To those who argued, then, that plays appealed only to unworthy members of society, Chapman answered that dramas were often supported by people of great distinction.

DEFENSES BASED ON PROFIT AND DELIGHT

From early in the 1500s (and even well before then), dramatists had been defending themselves by claiming that their art, by displaying examples of both good and bad behavior, taught worthy moral lessons. Thus George Gascoigne's *The Glass of Government* (1575) was described as a "tragical comedy so entitled because therein are handled as well the rewards for virtues as also the punishment for vices." Similar claims are extremely numerous. Thus a character in Francis Beaumont and John Fletcher's *The Triumph of Honor* (1608) asks his spouse, "What hurts now in a play, 'gainst which some rail so vehemently? Thou and I, my love, / Make excellent use, methinks: I learn to be / A lawful lover void of jealousy, / And thou a constant wife." Dramatists knew, of course, that they needed to write well and thus provide delight if they hoped to teach morality effectively. For this reason, they frequently justified theater's pleasures. Thus the drama *Locrine* (1595) claims to be "no less pleasant than profitable." Sometimes, though, plays were justified merely for providing innocent mirth. John Marston, for example, in *The Dutch Courtesan*, proclaimed that "if our pen in this [play] seem over slight, / We strive not to instruct, but to delight." But most dramatists pursued both aims to one degree or another.

SHAKESPEARE DEFENDS DRAMA

Shakespeare's own comments on drama can only be found in the speeches of his dramatic characters, making it difficult to know whether these comments reflect his own opinions. It is quite likely, however, Shakespeare agreed with Hamlet that "the purpose of playing" is "to hold, as 'twere, the mirror up to nature; to show virtue her own feature, scorn her own image, and the very age and body of the time his form and pressure" (3.2.20-24). Drama, in other words, should imitate reality, apparently to promote morality. Sometimes, however, Shakespeare seems to emphasize pleasure alone, as when Theseus, in *A Midsummer Night's Dream*, asks for a play "To ease the anguish of a torturing hour" (5.1.37) or when the physicians of a melancholy character in *The Taming of the Shrew* prescribe a play to "frame" his "mind to mirth and merriment, / Which bars a thousand harms and lengthens life" (Introduction, 2.135-16). This idea—that comedies could help promote health—was very common and was a principal way of defending drama. The surprising thing to us is that Shakespeare did not write more often or more openly about the art to which he had so clearly dedicated his life. Today the notion of needing to defend drama can seem surprising, but in Shakespeare's era attacks on plays, players, and play-making were so common that his relative silence on these matters seems all the more peculiar.

LONDON'S THEATERS
AND THEATER COMPANIES

Plays existed in England long before the rise of permanent, professional theaters. Earlier performances, however, had been infrequent, often special affairs put on either by amateurs on particular holidays or other unusual occasions or staged by traveling actors who moved from town to town and played wherever they could. Some plays were performed on carts; some were staged in the courtyards; some were presented in town halls or in large rooms within the homes or palaces of aristocrats or other notable people. Playing had not yet become fully professional, partly because the players had no real permanent homes.

Theaters in the modern sense—i.e., specially designed and designated buildings intended to be permanent and intended almost solely for the production of plays—apparently did not begin to appear in England until the 1560s and 1570s. As Herbert Berry notes, surviving records of the first such structure known to exist date from 1567; during the next two decades, at least 10 more were built. Suddenly London was the center of professional English theater, and a new capitalist, moneymaking enterprise had arisen. Along with theaters arose a radically transformed and much more settled, professional occupation: acting as a full-time way of making a living, with a stable location where one went to work each day.

Most public playhouses were built *outside* the formal boundaries of London—beyond its walls or across the Thames. By constructing most theaters in such places, their owners or operators thereby tried, not always successfully, to put them beyond the jurisdiction of London's mayor and aldermen—men who, as the preceding chapter showed, were often highly hostile to plays, playhouses, and players. Some theaters were eventually established within London itself, but they tended to be smaller, enclosed by walls and roofs, and thus more "private" than the open-air amphitheaters, such as the Globe, that we tend to associate with the great "public" theaters of Shakespeare's day. The "private" theaters charged higher admission prices and were in various other ways more exclusive than the open-air theaters, to which anyone could be admitted for a penny.

THE RED LION: 1567

The first public theater from which evidence survives was called The Red Lion. Herbert Berry calls it "the first structure now known to have been built as a regular professional theatre in the British Isles since Roman times." It lay about a mile east of London and was constructed at the behest of John Brayne, a grocer and the brother-in-law of James Burbage, later a great theatrical entrepreneur. The theater's design was simple, consisting mainly of a scaffold for spectators and a stage five feet off the ground measuring 40 feet by 30 feet and including a trapdoor. A "turret" rose 30 feet above the stage, although little else is known about this structure or the plays that may have been performed there. It seems to have existed only during the summer of 1567.

THE FOUR INNS: 1570S–'90S

Berry notes that four London inns were "among the earliest playhouses. . . . All opened for theatrical business in the 1570s, and all had ceased being playhouses, but continued as inns, by about 1596." He suggests that their "stages were, presumably, in their inn-yards, and their plays were performed in the open-air. Well-known companies of actors played at one time or another in them all." The inns were known as the Bel Savage, the Bull, the Cross Keys, and the Bell. All but one were in London and thus subject to the city's authority. Berry reports that "Virtually nothing is known for certain about either the ownership of these places or what was done to make them playhouses. Nor is much known about how their owners contrived to carry on theatrical enterprises for twenty years and more on the home ground of mayors and aldermen who disapproved of such things." At least one of these playhouses had a raised stage, places for spectators to stand, and a basic admission price of a penny—traits also associated with the later, more elaborate, and more famous theaters of Shakespeare's day. Fencing contests were also presented.

Even theater's great antagonist, Stephen Gosson, approved (in 1579) of some plays staged at the Bel Savage and the Bull, noting that two of these works featured "never a word without wit, never a line without pith, never a letter placed in vain," and praising two other plays for displaying neither an "amorous gesture wounding the eye, nor with slovenly talk hurting the ears of the chaste hearers." Indeed, Queen Elizabeth's own played at the Bull and the Bell, and the inn-playhouses often featured performances by Richard Tarlton, one of the greatest comic actors of the age. Even when the lord mayor attempted in1589 to suppress plays within London, he was defied at

Detail of "Long View of London from Bankside" from 1647. This etching is regarded as a very accurate portrayal of London during Shakespeare's time. The Globe Theatre is clearly labeled on the south side of the river. However, most scholars believe that the Globe was actually located in a different building, the one labeled "beer-bayting." In any case, this would have been the second Globe, which was rebuilt after the first burned down in 1613. *(Etching by Wenceslaus Hollar)*

the Cross Keys by some players patronized by Lord Strange. Meanwhile, the Bel Savage was supposed to have been the site at which the devil himself once appeared during the performance of a play about demons. As if this were not bad enough, one concerned mother by 1594 was warning a son about living so close to a theater "haunted with such pernicious and obscene plays"—a "theatre able to poison the very godly," not to mention her son's servants. According to one account, all four inn-theaters were abolished by the mid-1590s by the city authorities: These theaters were "put down and other lewd houses quite suppressed within the liberties [of the city] by the care of those religious senators." By 1600, the royal Privy Council itself decreed that there would be no more stage plays performed "in any common inn for public assembly in or near about the City."

THE PRIVATE PLAYHOUSE AT ST. PAUL'S CATHEDRAL: 1575–1606

St. Paul's Cathedral was by far London's largest church and was the most visible feature in its skyline. It dwarfed even the biggest parish churches surrounding it, and it was the city's crucial site for worship. It was also, however, a well-known meeting place, where people gossiped, did business (some of it illicit), and promenaded up and down the main aisle, wanting to see and to be seen. In some ways that main aisle was itself a theater, and so it is not surprising that an actual playhouse was established in a small building attached to the cathedral's south side. Its actors were, as Berry reports, "the ten boys who belonged to the [cathedral's] choir school and [who] were an important part of [its] musical establishment. Boys from the nearby St. Paul's grammar school may also have acted."

Berry notes that the "playhouse was apparently in the almonry [a small building from which alms were distributed to the poor], where the master of the choristers (who was also an almoner) lived along with, presumably, his charges." Sebstian Westcott helped supervise the choristers from 1559 to 1582, leading them (according to Berry) "in twenty-seven performances of plays at court, many more than any other [theatrical] companies of the time performed there." In 1584 Thomas Gyles succeeded Westcott, but even before this date the boys seem to have been playing not only at court but also within the almonry itself. In 1591, however, their performances suddenly ceased, for reasons not entirely clear, although the possibility that they were dealing with politically and religiously sensitive topics has been raised. Ironically, the playwrights who wrote for boy actors were notoriously more likely to deal with touchy subjects than those who wrote for adults. The plays staged by the boys were often sharply satirical, especially during the early 1600s.

By that point, under Edward Peers, playing by the boys of St. Paul's had been revived. One of their patrons and possible playwrights was the Earl of Derby. They resumed playing at court by early 1601. According to Berry, however, the "boys of St. Paul's apparently ceased performing plays professionally once and for all in the summer of 1606. They performed their last recorded play at court then, and, so far as direct evidence goes, they did not play publicly after that, either." The reasons they ceased playing are unknown, especially since their plays had proved highly popular (but also often highly controversial) and also since their playwrights included some of the best-known writers of the time. Their often satirical plays were part of the cutting edge of London's theatrical scene. Their plays were not staged in the large open-air amphitheaters, such as the famous Globe. Rather, they were put on for much smaller, more select audiences, both at court and at other such inside play spaces, including the small building attached to the cathedral itself.

THE THEATRE: 1576

The Theatre, a large, open-air structure, was erected just outside London's ancient northern walls at the instigation of James Burbage, a joiner who had become a professional actor. Berry notes that "The place opened before it was fully complete, probably in the latter half of [1576], and Burbage dominated its affairs until he died in 1597." Financing came partly from James Brayne, Burbage's brother-in-law, who had already helped found the Red Lion nine years earlier. The partners, however, were soon borrowing money from others and also soon quarreling with each other about the project's complicated financing. Despite these many difficulties, however, the Theatre was an enormous success.

Berry describes it as "a large timber building with tile roofs," with "a yard, tiring-house [i.e., room in which actors dressed and otherwise prepared], galleries in which spectators sat and stood, and a door leading up to the galleries at which a gatherer stood to take money from people going to the galleries." One foreign tourist noted that it had three galleries, one atop the other. A preacher in 1578 described it as a "gorgeous playing place," although another document from the same period makes clear that it was also used for exhibitions of swordsmanship. The Theatre was the direct ancestor of the first Globe, the playhouse Shakespeare made famous. Shakespeare himself acted at the Theatre, but not long after its construction, its plays were coming under attack. In 1577, for example, John Northbrooke called the Theatre (and another playhouse, The Curtain) a "spectacle and school for all wickedness and vice to be learned in." Ironically, however, even Stephen Gosson, a great enemy of most drama, conceded in 1579 that occasionally some performances at the Theatre were of "good plays and sweet plays."

Yet the Theatre continued to come under various assaults. In 1580, for instance, it was criticized by local officials as an alleged focus of "illicit assembly of people, great affrays, reviling, tumult and near insurrections, and divers other malefactions and enormities . . . perpetrated by a great many ill-disposed people in great disturbance of the peace of our lady the Queen, and also subversion of good order and government." Later, London's lord mayor was reporting to a top royal official that "on Sunday last some great disorder was committed at the Theatre," even noting that he had also sent "for the players to have appeared before" him since "those plays do make assemblies of citizens and their families" for whom the mayor was legally responsible.

In 1584 another city official reported that "Upon Wednesday, one Browne, a serving man in a blue coat, a shifting fellow having a perilous wit of his own, intending a spoil [i.e., theft or brawl] if he could have brought it to pass, did at [the] Theatre door quarrel with certain poor boys, handicraft apprentices, and struck some of them, and lastly he with his sword wounded and maimed one of the boys upon the left hand. Whereupon there assembled near . . . 1,050 people. This Browne did very cunningly convey himself away, but . . . he was taken after." Four days later, royal and civil authorities issued orders that the Theatre and another playhouse should be demolished, but Burbage, owner of the Theatre, stoutly resisted, and nothing further seems to have happened. The Theatre, then—like various other playhouses—was often seen by local authorities as a site of chaos and disorder. Not only did plays themselves often bother opponents of Elizabethan theater; so did disruptive offstage activities.

Many surviving documents about the Theatre concern the complex finances of its backers. Tensions and legal conflicts eventually led to a dramatic decision: Cuthbert Burbage, son of James, had the entire structure suddenly dismantled in late December 1598. Its timbers were taken across the Thames and were used to construct the brand-new Globe playhouse—site of many of Shakespeare's greatest theatrical triumphs. Thus the Theatre in a sense survived even after being deliberately torn down—a fact that only enhances its already great importance. The Theatre had probably hosted the premieres of a number of Shakespeare's early plays, including *Love's Labor's Lost*, *Richard II*, *Romeo and Juliet*, *A Midsummer Night's Dream*, *King John*, *The Merchant of Venice*, both parts of *Henry IV*, and *Much Ado About Nothing*.

THE CURTAIN: 1577

The Curtain was a public playhouse just north of the city and not far from the Theatre. According to Berry, "it probably opened in the autumn of 1577

. . . [and] remained in theatrical use longer than any other Shakespearean playhouse, from 1577 to 1625, and evidently was still standing in 1698." Its name, he continues, "had nothing to do with theatrical curtains. The pasture [in which the theater was situated] had been called the Curtain, meaning that it was enclosed by a wall, long before the playhouse existed." The person or people who "built the playhouse," Berry notes, "and how he, she, or they financed it are unknown, as is its ownership for most of its history." It was one of the first major amphitheaters erected in London and specifically designed for performances of plays. Like the Theatre, it had many sides, rather than being rectangular or square, and thus appeared "round," and also like the Theatre, it consisted of three stacked galleries surrounding a yard in which spectators stood before a raised stage.

According to Berry, the "Curtain was never one of the great playhouses. Its use is as imperfectly known as its ownership. No company [of players] is definitely known to have played there during the first twenty years, though Lord Arundel's men were probably there in 1584. Three companies are known to have used it for only about five of the next twenty-eight years. After the Lord Chamberlain's men abandoned the Theatre in the autumn of 1598, they played at the Curtain until they moved into the Globe in May 1599." Evidence suggests that the Curtain was used intermittently as a playhouse, by various companies, until 1625, and Berry even suggests that one reason we know so little about this house is that it was not the subject of continuous legal disputes (as the Theatre definitely was). John Northbrooke attacked it and the Theatre in late 1577 for offering homes for "vain plays" and "other idle pastimes" and for functioning as schools for "wickedness and vice to be learned in."

Indeed, Berry notes that "the Theatre and Curtain were often mentioned together." Thus in 1579 an anonymous critic ("T.F.") called attention to "the Theatres, Curtains, . . . bowling alleys, and such places where time is so shamefully misspent, namely [i.e., particularly] the Sabbath days, unto the great dishonor of God and the corruption and utter destruction of youth." He later called the Curtain and Theatre "two places . . . well known to be enemies to good manners," while John Stubbes in 1583 called them "Venus' palace and Satan's synagogue." Later that same year, a London official commented on the "profane spectacles at the Theatre and Curtain and other like places," while in 1587 another critic asserted that "The Theatre and Curtain may aptly be termed for their abomination the chapel of adultery."

In July 1597 the royal Privy Council ordered that both the Theatre and the Curtain be immediately demolished because of the "very great disorders committed in the common playhouses, both by lewd matters that are handled on the stages and by resort and confluences of bad people." The owners of the Curtain were expected to "pluck down quite the stages, galleries and rooms that are made for people to stand in, and so to deface the same as they may not be employed again to such use." For reasons unknown, this order was not carried out, and the Curtain survived, in one form or another, for another hundred years. Indeed, in the fall of 1599 a Swiss tourist, Thomas Platter, described in great detail seeing a comedy there featuring a competition between an Englishman and men of other nations. The Englishman eventually triumphed, of course, but Platter was nevertheless amused. He especially noted that when the play ended, the actors "danced very elegantly both in English and in Irish fashion."

Platter's report of visiting the Curtain, which was not far from the inn where he was staying, is especially interesting for its account of the general theatrical scene in the English capital: "every day at two o'clock in the afternoon in . . . London two and sometimes three comedies are performed at separate places wherewith folk make merry together, and whichever [theater] does best gets the greatest audience. The places are so built that they play on a raised platform, and everyone can well see it all. There are, however, separate galleries and there one stands more comfortably and, moreover, can sit, but one pays more for it. Thus anyone who remains on the level standing pays only one English penny. If he desires to sit on a cushion in the most comfortable place of all, where he not only sees everything well but can also be seen, then he gives yet another English penny at another door. And in the pauses of the comedy, food and drink are carried round amongst the people, and one can thus refresh himself at his own cost." During Platter's visit, the Curtain was one of London's top two open-air playhouses. Little more than a decade later, however, it was described disdainfully by the Venetian ambassador as "a place as dubious as they come, and where you would never see the face of a gentleman, let alone a nobleman."

THE ROSE: 1587

"The Rose," Berry remarks, "was the first of the five public playhouses built on Bankside in Southwark, near the south bank of the Thames." It opened in the fall of 1587 under the management of Philip Henslowe, a highly successful theatrical entrepreneur and a man whose "diary" provides crucial information about the daily theatrical business. The Rose's recently unearthed foundations suggest, as Berry notes, that it "was a timber-frame building originally of thirteen or fourteen somewhat irregular sides and [thus] could be seen as round. It may have been some 73 feet across and so probably smaller" than some other contemporary theaters. Like a number of the other open-air amphitheaters, it consisted, according to Berry, "of three tiers of galleries one above the other, the lowest about fourteen feet deep, around an open yard perhaps 45 feet across. The stage was on the northern side of the yard and was evidently unroofed. It was nearly 37 feet wide at the widest, tapered to about 27 feet at the front, and extended about 16 feet 6 inches into the yard."

Interestingly, the "northern half of the yard sloped downward toward the stage, probably to give spectators at the back a better view and to drain water to a wooden drain that began under the stage and led away north towards a ditch." If this feature was used in other amphitheaters, such as Shakespeare's Globe, visibility for "the groundlings" (the people who paid a penny to stand in the yard) may have been better than has often been assumed. In any case, Berry suggests that the "tiring house [where actors attired themselves] was apparently in the lower gallery behind the stage," and he also reports that from "February to April 1592 Henslowe spent well over £100 enlarging the Rose so that it could hold many more people," making the theater more egg-shaped than circular. By this point, too, two more rooms were constructed over the tiring house—the top of them being a "lord's room" where prominent visitors could easily be seen by other spectators. The stage itself was made more rectangular, and by 1595 (if not earlier) a roof covered the stage. Among many famous dramas staged here were Christopher Marlowe's *Tamburlaine*, *The Jew of Malta*, and *Dr. Faustus*, along with Thomas Kyd's ever-popular revenge play *The Spanish Tragedy*. The Rose may or may not have been demolished in 1606.

THE SWAN: 1595

Less than a decade after the Rose became the first public amphitheater built in Southwark, it was joined by the Swan, whose builder, Francis Langley, already owned an important "bear-garden," in which people paid to see dogs fight with chained bears. A Dutch visitor called the Swan "the largest and most distinguished" of the theaters surrounding London. "He said," as Berry puts it, that "it held 3,000 spectators and that its posts were skillfully painted to look like marble." This same Dutchman also made a famous sketch showing the inside of the Swan. Berry notes that in "the picture the Swan is round and consists mainly of three tiers of galleries, one over the other, surrounding an open yard. Interrupting the galleries and rising over them is a tiring-house, [or] . . . house of the players. A rectangular stage extends from the tiring-house perhaps half-way across the yard, so that spectators could stand on three sides of it." The Swan was thus entirely typical of the various other open-air amphitheaters.

Ironically, despite the Swan's grandeur, by the fall of 1598 it was no longer used, for a dozen years, as a place for routinely staging plays. Berry notes that "Playing went on again there from 1610 to 1614, and from 1620 to 1621, when it ended altogether," so that the "Swan had been a regular playhouse for only nine years." The reasons for these long interruptions are unclear. Even before the Swan was built, the City of London was objecting to its construction, but in 1596 an aristocratic German tourist described it as one of four local playhouses (including the Theater, the Curtain, and the Rose) "In which people counterfeit princes, kings, [and] emperors; / In fitting greatness of life, [and] in splendor of beautiful garments." Around the same time, the visiting Dutchman Johannes de Witt called all four theaters structures "of obvious beauty," but he was especially impressed with the Swan, terming it "the largest and most distinguished."

Yet the Swan was used not only for plays; a document from 1598 indicates that it was also the site of a competitive display in which the poet Robert Wilson showcased his ability to concoct numerous English verses extemporaneously—a talent that won him strong contemporary praise. The Swan was also the site, in 1602, of a famous deception in which a con man had promised a spectacular play, collected the money for it, and then absconded. According to letter writer John Chamberlain, "the common people, when they saw themselves deluded, revenged themselves upon the hangings, curtains, chairs, stools, walls and whatsoever came in their way, very outrageously, and made great spoil." But Chamberlain also notes that "a great store of good company [i.e., respected people], and many noblemen" were also present, and the hoax remained famous for many years. Also in 1603, the Swan featured a fencing contest in which one fencer "had so ill luck that the other ran him into the eye with a foil [i.e., a blunt-pointed rapier] and so far into the head that he fell down stark dead and never spake word nor once moved." In Elizabethan theaters, not only the plays were often shocking.

THE FIRST GLOBE: 1599

The first Globe playhouse, because of its strong association with Shakespeare, may be the most famous theater in the whole history of drama. Like the Rose and the Swan, it was built in Southwark, a suburb across the Thames from London. Theatergoers could access these playhouses by crossing the magnificent London Bridge or by being ferried across in narrow,

THE GLOBE THEATRE.

This structure must have been erected previous to the year 1563, as it is represented in a Plan of London, published during that year, but excluded in another plan, published from actual survey, in 1600, though it is known that many of Shakespeare's plays were performed in it at subsequent periods.— Stow records the destruction of this Theatre, during the year 1613, in a particular manner. He says, "Upon St.Peter's day last, the playhouse, or theater, called the Globe, upon the Banck side, neere London, by negligent discharging of a peale of ordinance, close to the South side thereof, the Thatch tooke fier, and the wind sodainly desperst the flame round about, and in a very short space the whole building was quite consumed, and no man hurt. The house being filled with people, to behold the play, viz. of Henry the 8.th And the next Spring it was new builded in far fairer manner then before." – Ben Jonson calls the Globe Theatre the 'Glory of the Bank' and the 'Fort of the whole parish.'

London, Published Oct.r 21st.st 1810 by Rob.t Wilkinson, 37.55, Cornhill. 170

The Globe Theatre. A detail of Wenceslaus Hollar's engraving, published by Robert Wilkinson in 1810.

long boats by watermen. Owned in part by some of the actors themselves (including Shakespeare, who, as a "sharer," was entitled to share in profits from admission fees), the Globe soon hosted first productions of some of the most famous plays ever written, for Shakespeare was, of course, not only an actor but a major playwright.

Interestingly enough, the Globe was constructed largely from timber that had once been part of the Theatre, the amphitheatre built outside London's northern walls. When that playhouse was pulled down, much of the lumber was hauled across the Thames, where the Globe was put up essentially across the street from the Rose. The Globe probably strongly resembled the Theatre in its basic shape and size. A nearly circular building, its diameter was between 80 and 100 feet, with the standard three galleries, the standard yard surrounding the stage that thrust out into the middle of the yard, and the same general capacity as the Theatre, with room for roughly 3,000 tightly packed spectators. Anyone who could pay the extra price could sit in the galleries, but the people who could afford only a penny stood around the stage, very close to the speeches and action. The stage was partly covered; a tiring-house was behind it; and the galleries were covered with thatch, which would eventually prove the Globe's undoing when a fire in the thatch in 1616 burned the theater to the ground.

One of the first—and few—records of an actual performance at the Globe comes from the report of Thomas Platter, a Swiss visitor who in the early autumn of 1599 described seeing a play there about Julius Caesar, which was "with at least fifteen characters very pleasingly acted." At the end "they danced, according to their custom, exceedingly gracefully: two attired in men's clothes and two in women's performed wonderfully with one another." Few other reports survive concerning the Globe in the first decade of its existence, when many of Shakespeare's plays were being

The rebuilt Globe Theatre in London. This photograph was taken in January of 2008. *(Used under a Creative Commons license)*

performed there. A poem from 1610 mocks a satirical out-of-town visitor to London who is obsessed with seeing plays and who visits various theaters, including the Globe. Meanwhile, a report from April 1610 noted that a visiting German prince "went to the Globe, the ordinary place where they play comedies, and there the story of the Moor of Venice [probably Shakespeare's *Othello*] was presented." Another German prince visited the Globe in 1611,

MASQUES

By the time of Shakespeare's death in 1616, masques had developed from relatively simple beginnings into highly elaborate forms of aristocratic entertainment. They typically involved music, dancing, and dramatic poetry, usually centering on the monarch and often performed on important occasions at the royal court, especially during the winter holidays. The earliest forms of such entertainment had been called "mummings," in which masked and costumed dancers approached the monarch, often to present symbolic gifts. Speeches were later added to these kinds of entertainments, and during the reign of King James the masques became especially fully developed thanks to the efforts of such talented poets as Ben Jonson and such gifted costume and set designers as Inigo Jones. A typical collaboration between Jonson and Jones involved an antimasque (usually emphasizing some kind of discord or disorder, often of a crude or comic sort). This was followed by a shift to harmony and order in the masque proper, which typically emphasized the benign, inspiring influence of the monarch. Professional actors often appeared in the antimasque; costumed aristocrats danced (frequently with members of the audience) in the masque itself. Masques increasingly dealt with important political and social issues of the day, sometimes offering implied criticism of government policies and often offering subtle counsel on significant current topics. Masques have occasionally been dismissed as examples of extravagant and expensive flattery of the monarch, but recent scholarship has suggested that they were often far more complicated in their meanings and implications. Participation in masques was an important form of self-display for Elizabethan and Jacobean courtiers, and mere attendance at masques was itself a sign of social rank. Masques were a way for the court to display its magnificence not only to itself but also to the foreign ambassadors who were almost inevitably in attendance. All eyes were not only on the masque but also on the monarch, who was always the most important member of the audience.

"Come now; what masques, what dances shall we have,
To wear away this long age of three hours
Between our after-supper and bed-time?"
— A *Midsummer Night's Dream* (5.1.32-35)

with a contemporary report calling this playhouse "the most important" of London's theaters. Unfortunately, just two years later the Globe was utterly destroyed by fire, although it was almost immediately rebuilt.

In a famous letter, Sir Henry Wotton described the incident. He reported that during a performance of Shakespeare's play *Henry VIII* on June 29, 1613, the fictional king Henry presented a masque [i.e., an elaborate musical and dramatic entertainment] "at the Cardinal Wolsey's house, and certain chambers [i.e., parts of a gun] being shot off at his entry, some of the paper or other stuff wherewith one of them was stopped did light [i.e., alight] on the thatch, where being thought at first but an idle smoke, and their eyes more attentive to the show, it kindled inwardly and ran round like a train [i.e., of gunpowder], consuming within less than an hour [another report says less than two hours] the whole house to the very grounds. This was the fatal period [i.e., end] of that virtuous fabric wherein yet nothing did perish but wood and straw and a few forsaken cloaks. Only one man had his breeches set on fire that would perhaps have broiled him if he had not by the benefit of a provident wit put it out with bottle ale." Yet another letter noted that "the people escaped all without hurt except one man who was scalded with the fire by adventuring to save a child which otherwise had been burned." The fact that the Globe was quickly reconstructed and improved implies how valuable it was, both financially and otherwise.

THE SECOND BLACKFRIARS: 1576, 1596, 1609

The "second" Blackfriars playhouse is so called because of an unsuccessful first attempt to establish an indoor playhouse, for adult actors, in a building that had originally been part of an old Dominican monastery in London. Boy players had performed there, before small and select audiences, for eight years beginning in 1576, but in 1596 James Burbage, the theatrical entrepreneur who ran the open-air Theatre, bought the property. He planned to turn part of it into a private, enclosed playhouse, especially since his lease on the property on which the Theatre stood was due to expire in 1597. Objections from prominent residents living near the Blackfriars building, who feared the increased noise and traffic an indoor adult playhouse might cause, scotched Burbage's original plans. Instead, the Theatre's timbers were moved across the river and were used to construct the first Globe. Meanwhile, parts of the Blackfriars building were apparently once again used, for the next 10 years or so, as a site for less bothersome performances by boys.

In 1608, the great adult actor Richard Burbage, son of the now-deceased James, joined with other members of his acting company, including Shakespeare, to open a new Blackfriars playhouse, as his father had originally planned. It was an indoor theater for adult actors and functioned, in essence, as the indoor home of the actors who regularly performed at the outdoor Globe. The new theater, which opened in 1609, thus allowed them to perform all year, even in winter weather. The second Blackfriars theater was in a different building of the old monastery than the first. "It was," says Berry, therefore "a much grander place than the first. It was probably a great deal higher—the height of at least two rooms built one over the other at the northern end—

Portrait of Richard Burbage, the leading performer of Shakespeare's company. *(ca. 1600, artist unknown)*

and its ceiling could have been a hammer beam roof . . . . At floor level it measured 66 feet north to south and 46 east to west. It comprised, therefore, 3,036 square feet, more than two and a half times the size of the first [Blackfriars theater]."

Berry suggests that the stage was at the southern end, although he doubts the common assumption that it was proscenium arch in design (i.e., not jutting out into the audience, as in the outdoor theaters). "Below the level of the stage," he continues, "there was a pit where people sat on benches. Somewhere there was a tiring-house. There were galleries, perhaps a single level of them, running around three sides of the room above the pit. There were boxes adjacent to and on a level with the stage, perhaps at the back. The stage was famous for the spectators on it, standing, sitting (on three-legged stools) and even reclining. But its size and shape are unknown." The Blackfriars, like other indoor playhouses, was especially likely to attract wealthy playgoers who wanted not only to see but also to be seen, not simply within the theater but even on the stage. Such self-display had already been common in playhouses where boys performed (such as the Blackfriars itself before the adults took over). The importance of the second Blackfriars is that it was, in Berry's words, "the first private playhouse in which adult players regularly performed."

Admission prices were higher than those for the open-air amphitheaters, and audiences were therefore smaller and more elite. Yet it is crucial to remember that Shakespeare's company, for years (beginning in 1609), performed both at the outdoor Globe *and* at the indoor Blackfriars. Their plays—even before but especially after the adults occupied the second Blackfriars—thus had to appeal to a very broad social spectrum, from poor commoners to the wealthy, educated social elite.

THE FIRST FORTUNE (1600) AND OTHER THEATERS

Various other playhouses existed in London during Shakespeare's lifetime, including the "first" Fortune theater, another open-air theater constructed in 1600 not far from London's northwestern boundaries. It was owned by Philip Henslowe and Edward Alleyn, two key figures in the London theatrical scene, and although its construction was overseen by Peter Street, who had also recently supervised construction of the first Globe, the first Fortune was unusual in being square in shape, rather than nearly round. Like the other amphitheaters, it had a stage jutting into a yard, and the yard itself was surrounded by three galleries, although in this case each gallery was wider by 10 inches than the one below it. A play probably performed at the Fortune about a decade after the playhouse opened has a character describe the surrounding

> Storeys of men and women mixed together,
> Fair ones with foul, like sunshine in wet weather.
> Within a square a thousand heads are laid
> So close that all of heads the room seems made.
> As many faces there (filled with blithe looks)
> Show like the promising titles of new books . . . .
>
> And here and there (whilst with obsequious ears
> Thronged heaps do listen) a cutpurse thrusts and leers
> With hawks' eyes for his prey.

Various other playhouses were open for business in or near London during Shakespeare's lifetime, including Newington Butts, the Boar's Head, the Whitefriars, the Red Bull, and the Hope. But comments such as the one quoted above remind us that the most important aspect of Elizabethan theaters was not the buildings themselves but what went on inside them, both onstage and off.

ACTING COMPANIES

Companies of actors—both boys and adults—arose, developed, changed, and often disappeared over time. Sometimes one company would merge with another; sometimes it would split; and, in one famous case—when Queen Elizabeth decided to patronize a company of her own—the best actors from several existing companies suddenly became the Queen's Men. Aristocrats often sponsored companies that would frequently travel throughout the country or throughout specific areas; such companies advertised the power and extended the influence of their patrons. It was in London, however, that various companies began to find regular homes in theaters. Andrew Gurr is the best contemporary authority on all these matters, as on so much else concerning the Elizabethan theater. He notes, for instance, that a boys' company had found a regular indoor playing place in the Blackfriars district by 1576, although it had lost that place by 1584 and thereafter ceased playing. In that same year, however, boys associated with St. Paul's began performing, often at the court itself, although eventually their activities also ceased.

Various adult companies rose and fell in the last two decades of the sixteenth century, including the Earl of Worcester's Men, the Lord Admiral's Men, Lord Strange's Men, and the Lord Chamberlain's Men—the company to which Shakespeare belonged. Actors, especially lead actors, often moved from one company to another, and different companies sometimes moved to new theaters. Both kinds of movement were usually financially motivated. By 1594 the Queen's Men had ceased to exist, leaving the Admiral's Men and the Lord Chamberlain's Men as the two most important London companies in the latter 1590s and into the 1600s. Shakespeare was not only an actor for the Lord Chamberlain's Men but, under a new system, one of its actual "sharers," or co-owners. It was this arrangement, rather than his acting or playwriting, that eventually made him wealthy. He and various colleagues ultimately owned the two most important London playhouses: the Globe (an amphitheater built in 1599) and the Blackfriars (an indoor hall occupied in 1609). Profits benefited a company's sharers directly. When King James succeeded Queen Elizabeth in 1603, the Lord Chamberlain's Men became the King's Men—the most famous and important company in the land.

For Shakespeare and his comrades, the main competition from other adult actors came mostly from the Admiral's Men, who played mainly at the Fortune, outside London's northern walls. Yet all the adult actors soon had to compete, at least temporarily, with two different companies of boys: those associated with St. Paul's, who were up and running again in 1599, and a group called the Chapel Children, established in 1600 and playing in a hall in the Blackfriars district. (An attempt by Shakespeare's adult company to play there had been squelched by powerful neighbors, who feared the noise and congestion an adult theater might cause.) Plays written for the boys' companies were often satirical, sometimes involving personal mockery. The boys' patrons were also usually wealthier and better educated than many attendees at the amphitheaters. Competitive tensions between the different kinds of companies sometimes boiled over into the phrasing of the plays written for them. By the middle to latter years of the new century's first decade, however, the boys' companies had either ceased playing altogether or had ceased being major features of the theatrical scene. For most London audiences, it was and always had been the adult players who commanded the most attention.

AUDIENCES IN SHAKESPEARE'S TIME

Many contemporary anecdotes, gathered by Gurr, depict the theaters as lively, intriguing, often unpredictable places where some of the most interesting actions were performed by the audiences themselves. Thus Sir John Davies, in a satirical epigram from around 1593, described how a

> Courtier, at the Theater,
> Leaving the best and most conspicuous place,
> Doth either to the stage himself transfer,
> Or through a grate, doth show his double face,
> For that the clamorous fry of Inns of Court [i.e., law students]
> Fills up the private rooms of greater price:
> And such a place where all may have resort,
> He in his singularity doth despise.

In other words, it wasn't enough for this courtier to be seen conspicuously along with others who also wanted to be seen: He had to make himself even more singularly visible. For many members of the audience, the theater was as much a place for self-display as for witnessing the performances of others—performances that took place both onstage and off. A few years later Ben Jonson mocked the kind of disapproving "gallant" who, in order "to be thought one of the judicious," would sit conspicuously "with his arms thus wreathed, / His hat pulled here," and would cry out and nod and then shake "his empty head." Yet alongside such obvious fault finders one could also observe, in the words of the dramatist John Day, groups of a playwright's friends—"a prepared company of gallants, to applaud his jests, and grace out his play." Playhouses, then, often functioned partly as fields of competition between different playgoing factions.

THE SOCIAL COMPOSITION OF THE AUDIENCES

Theater historians have long debated the nature of Shakespeare's audiences. Some, such as Alfred Harbage, suggested that Shakespeare wrote mainly for "groundlings"—poorer people who paid a penny for admission to the amphitheaters (such as the Globe) and who literally stood on the ground, surrounding the elevated stage on three sides. Later scholars, especially Ann Jennalie

Cook, argued that Elizabethan dramatists wanted to appeal especially to "privileged playgoers," who were better-educated, had more leisure time, and could afford to sit in the higher-priced galleries surrounding the stage, although more distant from it. These people, arguably, could best appreciate Shakespeare's often splendid writing, with its frequently complex language, clever allusions, witty wordplay, and sometimes weighty intellectual content. These "privileged playgoers" inevitably exercised great social power. Their opinions of a play or playwright probably counted most, particularly to the aspiring playwrights themselves. Privileged audience members were socially influential in ways that "groundlings" simply were not. Of course, "groundlings" paid their pennies, which added up. Thus the economic importance of those who stood rather than sat can never be dismissed. They helped the theaters survive and thrive, especially the large amphitheaters. (The smaller, enclosed halls were more socially and economically exclusive: Audiences in the halls were not only all seated but were also far more definitely "privileged" than the larger, more heterogeneous groups who filled the amphitheaters.)

Andrew Gurr sides slightly more with Cook's emphasis on "privileged playgoers" than with Harbage's focus on "groundlings." Yet Gurr stresses the topic's enormous complexity and the need to speak as precisely as possible about *particular* theaters at particular points in history. He stresses the difference between plays written for the smaller, more exclusive "halls" and the larger, more inclusive amphitheaters. Some plays, however, were eventually performed in both kinds of venues. This was especially true of dramas staged by Shakespeare's company after it opened the second Blackfriars theater in 1609. Therefore, even broad generalizations about differences between the audiences for the amphitheaters and the halls must sometimes be significantly qualified.

INSIDE THE PLAYHOUSES

Gurr notes that in the amphitheaters it typically cost one penny to stand around the stage, two to sit in the galleries, and six to sit in the so-called "lords' rooms" built above the tiring-house at the rear of the stage. The occupants of these rooms were highly visible, although their own view of the play was ironically less complete than the views of those who paid less. Gurr estimates that 800 people could cram into the typical amphitheater yard and 2,000 into the tight-fitting galleries, with no more than around 700 able to fit, altogether, into the largest indoor halls. (The indoor theater at St. Paul's may have been able to hold fewer than 200 people.) Ironically, at the outdoor amphitheaters the people who paid least were closest to the stage, whereas the opposite was true in the halls. In the halls, especially privileged playgoers could typically pay to sit or otherwise relax on the stage itself, behind or to the sides of performing players. Amphitheater plays generally began at 2 p.m., when light was abundant, although even the indoor hall plays also usually started at this time. Plays often lasted about three hours, especially in the halls, since pauses were needed so candles could be trimmed.

Gurr suggests that the poorest playgoers who wanted to see performances at the amphitheaters on the south bank crossed London Bridge for free, whereas wealthier persons crossed the river in numerous boats resembling modern taxis. Gurr also estimates that in Shakespeare's day there was a theater of some sort within two miles of every London citizen. Indeed, when wealthy people began using carriages to get to the playhouses (especially the indoor halls), traffic jams often resulted. Apparently people were willing to attend plays no matter what the weather, even standing in the rain in the amphitheaters. Gurr argues, however, that actually hearing all the words spoken onstage was probably a greater problem than bad weather. Outdoor performances went on without breaks, although refreshments—mainly nuts, apples, water, and bottled ale—were often consumed, as popcorn and soft drinks are consumed in movie theaters today. If a theatergoer had to defecate, the Thames was nearby; if he or she needed to urinate, buckets were available, and some women even apparently carried small containers under their skirts.

Gurr depicts the outdoor theaters as ripe with strong smells, including odors from perfume, spicy food, and tobacco. (The smell of human perspiration must also have been powerful, since deodorants were nonexistent, nor did people wash as often or as thoroughly as today.) He quotes the playwright John Marston, who in 1600 commented on the odors and crowding of the open-air theaters, where a person was likely to be "choked / With the stench of garlic" and might even be "pasted / To the barmy [i.e., froth-covered] jacket of a beer-brewer." Six years later, writer Thomas Dekker similarly described how the open-air playhouses "smoked every afternoon with stinkards who were so glued together in crowds with the steams of strong breath that when they came forth, their faces looked as if they had been parboiled." As if the smells were not bad enough, Gurr says that many theatergoers wore hats during performances, thus somewhat obstructing the views of those behind them, and he suggests that the amphitheaters were much noisier than the halls.

AUDIENCES INDOORS AND OUT

Outdoor plays appealed to numerous spectators, including the illiterate or unemployed, as well as many apprentices, servants, masters, mistresses, and other social superiors, even the wealthy or aristocrats. Other citizens of London, such as shop owners and other merchants, attended, too, but were more likely to visit the open-air theaters than the private halls. In the amphitheaters especially, the audience probably reflected a real diversity of backgrounds, classes, and professions, whereas audiences in the halls were composed mainly of people from the upper end of the social spectrum. Gurr suggests that members of the gentry—landowners and other wealthy people who were not nobles or aristocrats—attended both indoor and outdoor theaters in significant numbers. Many women apparently went to plays both inside and outside (they are mentioned frequently in documents from the time), although women were expected to be escorted by men to avoid being perceived as prostitutes. Young lawyers and law students were perhaps more likely to attend the indoor theaters, especially as time wore on, although they were apparently quite a presence in outdoor theaters in the 1590s, especially for plays with romantic plots (such as *Romeo and Juliet*).

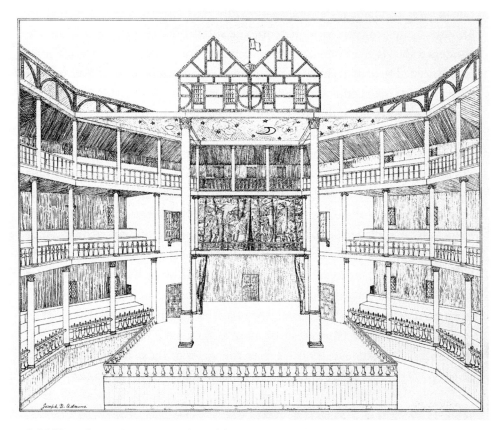

A 1922 conjectural reconstruction of Shakespeare's Globe Theatre. *(Drawing by Joseph Quincy Adams)*

Indeed, amphitheaters regularly attracted broad cross-sections of the population—perhaps more than any other routine events of the time. Much evidence from the period suggests that the open-air theaters provided opportunities for members of many different ranks, classes, and professions to intermingle. In 1609, for instance, Thomas Dekker noted that in the theaters, anyone with enough money could pay to sit on the stage and thus be seen by everyone else. The typical playhouse, he claimed, allowed "a stool as well to the farmer's son as to your Templar [i.e., lawyer or law student]: . . . your stinkard has the self-same liberty to be there in his tobacco-fumes, which your sweet courtier hath: and . . . your car-man [i.e., cart driver] and tinker claim as strong a voice in their suffrage [i.e., opinions], and sit to give judgment on the play's life and death, as well as the proudest *Momus* [i.e., critic]."

Even within the hall theaters, according to Ben Jonson, the relatively lowly could mingle with the socially pretentious if they could pay the six-penny price of admission. Thus he mocked

> The wise and many-headed bench, that sits
> Upon the life and death of plays and wits [e.g., playwrights],
> (Composed of *Gamester, Captain, Knight, Knight's man,*
> *Lady,* or *Pucell* (i.e., prostitute), that wears a mask or fan,
> *Velvet,* or *Taffeta* cap, ranked in the dark
> With the shop's *Foreman* or some such *brave spark* . . . .

Meanwhile, playwright Francis Beaumont remarked that half the audience who had originally condemned his friend John Fletcher's play *The Faithful Shepherdess* couldn't even read. Later, in another play, he had a character comment on the apprentices who were admitted to plays three to "a groat [i.e., shilling]," where they would "crack nuts with the scholars in the penny-rooms . . . and fight for apples." Even when performances had officially ended (according to an epigram by Sir John Davies), huge crowds gathered together outside:

> at all the play house doors,
> When ended is the play, the dance, the song,
> A thousand townsmen, gentlemen, and whores,
> Porters and serving-men together throng

Plays, especially in the amphitheaters, were occasions when many different kinds of people could mix and mingle, even when the main show itself had finished.

HEARING AND SEEING: AUDIENCES AND SPECTATORS

Although many members of the audiences attended plays throughout the period to hear well-written speeches and dialogue, spectacle—including striking costumes and memorable stage effects—also became increasingly important. Playwrights themselves, of course, generally valued words over actions and over other kinds of visual display, often alluding not only to well-known books (including the classics, the Bible, as well as more recent writings) but also to other contemporary plays. "Audiences," however, according to Gurr, increasingly became "spectators" as time wore on. They were more and more attracted by onstage action and other elements of spectacle, especially as the theaters became more mechanically sophisticated. Trapdoors allowed characters to appear and disappear suddenly; in the better amphitheaters, characters could be raised and lowered from pulleys housed in the roofs that partially covered the stage. But productions in Shakespeare's day featured none of the elaborate designs and lighting used in theaters today. The stage was mainly bare, except for a few important props. Elaborate costumes were often used, but performances then were generally more concerned with speeches and dialogue than is often the case today.

Playwrights often complained about the quality of audiences, especially in the amphitheaters. In 1606, for instance, John Day lamented that it was impossible to please everyone in a playhouse, especially if they failed to understand a playwright's intentions:

> Neither quick mirth, invective, nor high state,
> Can content all: such is the boundless hate
> Of a confused audience.

Similarly, in 1609 Ben Jonson praised the "quick [i.e., intelligent] ears" of audiences at court (who supposedly paid careful and thoughtful attention to his masques), even as he lamented the "sluggish" ears of audiences in the open-air theaters. These audiences, he groused, consisted of "porters and mechanics," whose ears had to be "bored through, at every act, with [explanatory] narrations." Later he complained that in the reception of many plays, "dances and antics" were usually "the only point of art that tickle[d]" most "spectators."

Jonson was hardly alone in such misgivings. Thus John Webster grumbled in 1612 that "most of the people that come to [the] playhouse, resemble those ignorant asses" who, when they visit bookshops, look not "for good books, but new books." Mere novelty, in other words, was often highly valued. Also in 1612, Thomas Dekker wished that audiences might be composed of the "very *Muses* themselves," or at least that they would be populated by "full, free, and *Knowing Auditor[s].*" Instead, according to John Fletcher in 1613, many people came to the theaters merely "to take their ease, / And sleep an hour or two," while others came to shout approval of personal satire of a kind that (Fletcher claimed) was never intended. Playwrights did, of course, appreciate applause, but they appreciated it most if it came from knowledgeable people.

AUDIENCE TASTES AND AUDIENCE REACTIONS

Audiences could often be quite demonstrative. They were particularly likely to respond, at least according to Stephen Gosson, to anything unusual, showy, or spectacular. Thus Gosson noted in 1596 that in the "public theaters, when any notable show passeth over the stage, the people arise in the seats, and stand upright with delight and eagerness to view it." Such behavior would be frowned upon today, but apparently it was not uncommon during the reigns of Elizabeth and James. Responses— whether positive or negative—tended to be strong, forceful, and sometimes even vocal. Poet Michael Drayton, for instance, described "thronged theaters" full of "shouts and claps at every little pause," while John Weever described, in a somewhat mixed metaphor, how "thousands" would "flock to hear a poet's pen" and how actors, to stir the audience emotions, would "make sighs a burden [i.e., musical accompaniment] for each sentence." Strong emotions, apparently, were frequently expressed, both onstage and off, and sometimes they were not entirely positive. Thus John Marston was only one of many people who commented on audiences' tastes for personal or otherwise biting satire (especially in the indoor halls). Marston wrote in 1601,

> This is the strain [i.e., kind of thing] that chokes the theaters:
> That makes them crack with full-stuffed audience,
> This is your humor [i.e., style] only in request:
> Forsooth to rail [i.e., make satirical attacks], this brings your ears to
>   bed,
> This people gape for, for this some doe stare.
> This some would hear, to crack the author's neck;
> This admiration and applause pursues.

John Day, in 1606, had a character directly address the audience and ask, in somewhat exasperated tones,

Alas, gentlemen, how is't possible to content you? You [perhaps addressing one part of the crowd] will have railing, and invectives, which our author neither dares, nor affects [i.e., aims at]; you [perhaps addressing another section] [desire] bawdy and scurrile jests, which neither becomes his modesty to write, nor the ear of a generous auditory to hear; you [perhaps addressing yet another part of the crowd] must have swelling comparisons, and bombast epithets, which are as fit for the body of a comedy as *Hercules*' shoe for the foot of a pigmy . . . .

It was impossible, Day suggested, to please everyone; audiences consisted of different factions with wildly varying tastes, and sometimes playwrights' attempts to meet the demands of some of those factions could get the writers themselves into trouble. This was especially true of the demand for personal satire, especially if the people satirized were socially or politically important. Official punishment for obviously personal satire was a real risk, but punishment might result as well, at least according to Francis Beaumont, for excessively racy material. Thus in a 1607 prologue Beaumont declared that

If there be any amongst you, that came to hear lascivious scenes, let them depart, for I do pronounce this, to the utter discomfort of all two-penny gallery men, you shall have no bawdry in it; or if there be any lurking amongst you in corners, with table books [i.e., notebooks], who have come to find fit matter to feed his malice on, let them clasp them up, and slink away, or stay and be converted. For he that made this play means to please auditors so as he may be an auditor himself hereafter, and not purchase them with the dear loss of his ears.

Few writers were ever actually punished by having their ears cut off, although some were so threatened. But more than one contemporary playwright mentioned punishment of a different sort: hostile responses (especially hissing) from disapproving spectators. Thus the essay writer John Stephens, in 1615, comically described a "base mercenary poet" who, "when he hears his play hissed, . . . would rather think bottle-ale is opening," while William Fennor, a year later, described how audiences, responding to one play, "screwed their scurvy jaws and looked awry, / Like hissing snakes adjudging it to die." In contrast, Fennor claimed, "wits of gentry did applaud the same, / With silver shouts of high loud-sounding fame: / While understanding grounded men [a possible reference to groundlings] condemned it." In either case, Fennor continued, "Clapping or hissing is the only mean[s] / That tries and searches out a well-writ *Scene* . . . / The stink-ards oft will hiss without a cause, / And for a bawdy jest will give applause. / Let but one ask the reason why they roar, / They'll answer, cause the rest did so before." Fennor seemed disgusted by such ignorant outbursts, but another writer claimed, a year later, that the players themselves were "much out of countenance, if fools do not laugh at them, boys [do not] clap their hands, peasants [do not] ope[n] their throats, and the rude rabble [do not] cry excellent, excellent."

"KNAVERY" AT THE PLAYHOUSES

However they reacted—whether with shouts, applause, or hissing—Eliza-bethan audiences apparently expressed themselves freely. In fact, it was at least as much audience conduct as the content of the plays that bothered some contemporary opponents of drama. Nevertheless, the playhouses flourished. Gurr cites a wonderful example of the mixed reactions theaters could provoke when he quotes from a 1578 book by John Florio designed to teach English to Italians. The book contains this snatch of memorable conversation:

> Where shall we go?
> To a play at the Bull, or else to some other place.
> Do comedies like you well?
> Yea sir, on holy days.
> They please me also well, but the preachers will not allow them.
> Wherefore, know you it:
> They say, they are not good.
> And wherefore are they used [i.e., why do they exist]?
> Because every man delights in them.
> I believe there is much knavery used at those comedies.
> So I believe also.

This dialogue, which today sounds splendidly stilted, is perhaps most intriguing because, although it concedes that comedies have been condemned by clerics, it nevertheless reports that "every man delights in them." Mean-while, it is by no means clear whether the "knavery" mentioned here refers to conduct onstage, offstage, or both. Even a basic defender of plays such as Henry Chettle admitted, in 1592, that behavior in the amphitheaters was often rowdy. He thus urged that "the young people of the city" should "either . . . abstain altogether from plays, or [should] at their coming thither use [i.e., behave] themselves after a more quiet order. In a place so civil as this city is esteemed, it is more than barbarously rude, to see the shameful disorder and routs [i.e., loud noises or shouts] that sometimes in such public meetings are used."

CRIME INSIDE AND OUTSIDE THE THEATERS

At least as shameful as such chaos, in Chettle's view, were the frequent thefts in playhouses: "The beginners" of disruptive commotions, Chettle claimed, were "neither gentlemen, nor citizens, nor any of both their servants, but some lewd mates that long for innovation." These connivers, he asserted, tried to provoke conflicts and even fights between rival groups so they could profit from the tumults: "when they see advantage, that either serving-men or apprentices are most in number, they will be of either side, though indeed they are of no side, but men beside all honesty, willing to make boot [i.e., booty] of cloaks, hats, purses, or whatever they can lay hold on in a hurly burly." Such disorders are mentioned fairly often in contemporary documents. Part of the excitement of going to some playhouses, then, may have been the simple prospect that battles would break out. Pickpockets, prostitutes, panderers, and con men saw opportunities in the large crowds, especially in the outdoor theaters, and sometimes thieves were apprehended by the audiences themselves and even punished by being tied to posts onstage. Usually, however, crimes at playhouses were carefully concocted so the criminals could make quick escapes. Thus, around 1595 an epigram by Sir John Harington described how two thieves plotted to accost a wealthy, well-dressed woman who was wearing rich jewels at the theater. Their plan was simple: While one distracted her by reaching under her dress, the other would "slip away" with her exposed jewelry.

An 1806 engraving of Francis Beaumont. *(Engraving by Samuel Freeman; print by George Vertue)*

DRESSING UP FOR PLAYS

As Harington's anecdote suggests, some attendees saw theaters as places for elaborate self-display, especially of fine clothing. Thus a Venetian reported in 1617 that the theaters were "frequented by a number of respectable and handsome ladies, who come freely and seat themselves among the men without the slightest hesitation." When he himself attended a play, he reported, some friends tricked him

> by placing me amongst a bevy of beautiful women. Scarcely was I seated ere a very elegant dame, but in a mask, came and placed herself beside me. . . . She determined to honor me by showing me some fine diamonds on her fingers, repeatedly taking off no fewer than three gloves, which were worn over the other. . . . This lady's bodice was of yellow satin richly embroidered, her petticoat of gold tissue with stripes, her robe of red velvet with a raised pile [i.e., nap on a fabric], lined with yellow muslin with broad stripes of pure gold. She wore an apron of point lace of various patterns: her head-tire was highly perfumed, and the collar of white satin beneath the delicately-wrought ruff struck me as extremely pretty.

Presumably the "trick" played on this man by his friends involved trying to arouse him in some way, in which case their plan seems to have worked.

Also in 1617, Robert Anton published a satirical poem mocking the "gilded clothes" that "swarms of wives" wore to the theaters, where, Anton claimed, these women often broke "their nuptial oaths." Apparently, however, it was by no means only females who liked to look attractive at playhouses. Thus a satirical pamphlet from 1620 describes a "Womanish-Man," who, before entering a theater, took "a full survey of himself, from the highest sprig in his feather to the lowest spangle that shines in his shoe-string." In contrast, court records from 1611 describe a woman (Marion Frith) who notoriously appeared at the Fortune "in man's apparel and in her boots and with a sword at her side." Apparently "she told the company then present that she thought many of them were of opinion she was a man, but if any of them would come to her lodging they should find she is a woman." Frith "also sat upon the stage in public view of all the people there present in man's apparel and played upon her lute and sang a song." Actors, it seems, were not the only ones in theaters who were concerned about their costuming and about putting on a show. Thus William Harison claimed in 1623 that "few of either sex come thither [i.e., to the theaters] but in the holiday apparel, and so set forth, so adorned, so decked, so perfumed, as if they made the place the market of wantonness, and by consequence too unfit for a priest to frequent." No wonder, then, that Harison also contended that "no true Puritans will endure to be present at plays."

WRITING FOR LONDON'S THEATERS

Although attacks on theater by civic authorities, Puritans, and other committed Christians were common in Shakespeare's day, playhouses obviously thrived. They were often very profitable indeed. Thousands of people—almost all of whom would have considered themselves genuine Christians and reasonably good citizens—visited playhouses repeatedly and apparently with clear consciences. Inevitably, opponents of theater were more vocal than people who simply paid for admission and enjoyed the shows. Playwrights, meanwhile, spent most of their time writing plays and earning money for doing so; they showed remarkably little interest in defending their profession. This fact is intriguing: It suggests that they felt little *need* to defend themselves, little real pressure to justify their craft. Players were regularly invited to perform at court; they were welcomed in towns and at large estates; and their dramas were admired and financially supported by a very broad cross-section of the English population, especially in London. Attacks on plays continued throughout Shakespeare's lifetime, but they were far less frequent after James succeeded than they had been earlier.

PLAYWRIGHTS AS CRITICS

Many discussions by playwrights on the nature of drama and writing have been helpfully collected in David Klein's *The Elizabethan Dramatists as Critics*. Klein quotes, for instance, dialogue from George Chapman's *The Revenge of Bussy d'Ambois* (published in 1613), in which a character extols drama's ability to realistically depict people at both the top and bottom ends of the social spectrum. The character concludes by maintaining that since both kinds of people are

> so easily borne [i.e., impersonated] by expert actors,
> The stage and actors are not so contemptful [i.e., worthy of contempt]
> As any innovating puritan
> And ignorant sweater-out of zealous envy
> Would have the world imagine.

Yet Chapman's character had already admitted, a few lines earlier, that not all contemporary plays deserved praise; he had conceded that unfortunately

we must have nothing brought on stages [now]
But puppetry and pied ridiculous antics.
Men thither [i.e., to the theater] come to laugh, and feed fool-fat,
Check all goodness there, as being profan'd . . .

Chapman, of course, obviously exempts his own play (and, by implication, various others) from such criticism, and indeed in dedicating it he asserted that "material instruction, elegant and sententious excitation to virtue, and deflection from her contrary" were "the soul, limbs and limits of an authentical tragedy."

Many dramatists, including Chapman, defended plays by noting that they had often been well received and encouraged by aristocrats and even royalty. In a rigidly hierarchical society, in which approval by a king or queen could easily trump the complaints of a Puritan, alderman, or lord mayor, such defenses recognized a very practical reality. They may not have been the best logical or theoretical arguments in favor of plays, but they could easily help intimidate and silence drama's opponents. Thus Chapman, in dedicating *The Widow's Tears* (ca. 1605), noted that "Other countrymen [i.e., people from other countries] have thought the like worthy of dukes' and princes' acceptations. *Ingiusti Sdegni, Il Patamento Amoroso, Calisto, Pastor Fido*, etc. (all being but plays) were all dedicate[d] to the princes of Italy." Criticism of plays does seem to have diminished whenever royals (especially James and his family) actively patronized drama. Thus the kind of argument Chapman makes here may actually have been more practically effective than more complicated theoretical defenses might have been.

THE MORALITY OF PLAYS

Some playwrights, as Chapman's dedication shows, defended their works by claiming that their plays promoted morality and discouraged evil. Thus Robert Wilmot, in a 1591 dedication of *Tancred and Sigismunda*, announced that its purpose lay in "commending virtue, detesting vice, and lively deciphering their overthrow that suppress not their unruly affections [i.e., passions]." The play, Wilmot asserted, tended "only to the exaltation of virtue and the suppression of vice." Later, at the conclusion of John Day's drama *The Parliament of Bees* (ca. 1608–16), a character praised art for having "banished ignorance, / And chased all flies of rape and stealth / From forth our winged commonwealth," while a character in an induction that John Webster wrote for John Marston's *The Malcontent* (1602) asserts that "such vices as stand not accountable to law should be cured as men heal tetters [i.e., skin pustules],—by casting ink upon them." Meanwhile, the playwright and former actor Nathaniel Field, in praising John Fletcher's *The Faithful Shepherdess* (performed circa 1608; published ca. 1609), extolled it for being "Clad in such elegant propriety / Of words, including a morality / . . . sweet and profitable." Chapman had already (in 1605) praised Ben Jonson's *Sejanus* by claiming that the play "hath this due respect / That it lets nothing pass without observing / Worthy instruction; or that might correct / Rude manners, and renown [i.e., make renowned] the well-deserving."

Sometimes the virtues plays encouraged and the vices they condemned were explicitly spelled out. Thus a character at the conclusion of *The Triumph of Honor* (ca. 1608–13), by Beaumont and Fletcher, turns to his spouse and asks,

> What hurts now in a play, 'gainst which some rail
> So vehemently? Thou and I, my love,
> Make excellent use, methinks: I learn to be
> A lawful lover void of jealousy,
> And thou a constant wife.

Likewise, in the same authors' tragicomedy *Philaster* (1612–13), the king ultimately urges "princes [to] learn / By this [play] to rule the passions in their blood; / For what Heaven wills can never be withstood." In *The Maid's Tragedy* (ca. 1610–11), also by Beaumont and Fletcher, a new ruler shows that he has learned well from his predecessor's mistakes: "May this a fair example be to me, / To rule with temper; for in lustful kings / Unlook'd-for sudden deaths from Heaven are sent." Whether the ethics plays taught were personal or political, many playwrights defended their works on moral grounds. Doing so was an especially effective justification during the English Renaissance. Thus Thomas Tomkis, in a play titled *Lingua* (ca. 1603), has a character proclaim that both comedy and tragedy "vice detect and virtue beautify, / By being death's mirror, and life's looking glass."

DRAMA AS A MIRROR OF LIFE

The idea that drama was a mirror held up to life was ancient—at least as ancient, as Klein notes, as the Roman statesman Cicero. The comparison was especially popular during Shakespeare's time, and it was Shakespeare himself, of course, who perhaps expressed it most memorably when he had Hamlet instruct some actors to

> Suit the action to the word, the word to the action, with this
> special observance, that you o'erstep not the modesty of nature:

for any thing so o'erdone is from the purpose of playing, whose end, both at the first and now, was and is, to hold as 'twere the mirror up to nature: to show virtue her feature, scorn her own image, and the very age and body of the time his form and pressure. (3.2.17-24)

Numerous other Elizabethan playwrights justified drama in exactly this way, as when John Marston, in the prologue to his 1604 play *The Fawn*, refers to "the nimble form [i.e., genre] of comedy" as a "Mere spectacle of life and public manners," while Nathaniel Field, in a prologue to his 1612 play A *Woman Is a Weathercock*, tells the "ignorant" reader that "a play is not so idle a thing as thou art, but a mirror of men's lives and actions."

HIDDEN MEANINGS

Even though the idea that drama was a mirror might imply that its meanings were obvious, Klein reminds us that some writers justified plays by claiming that they contained hidden but worthy meanings. These had to be sought or puzzled out by perceptive audiences and readers. Thus Nicholas Udall, in his play *Ralph Roister Doister* (probably written around 1553 but not published until 1567), proclaims in a prologue that

> The wise poets long time heretofore,
> Under merry comedies secrets did declare,
> Wherein was contained very virtuous lore,
> With mysteries and forewarnings very rare.

Likewise, the epilogue to another play from the mid-sixteenth century, *Jack Juggler* (author unknown), declares that "This trifling interlude that before you hath been rehearsed, / May signify some further meaning if it be well searched." Similar justifications of drama were offered by various later writers, including Thomas Lodge, Thomas Nashe, Thomas Heywood, and numerous others. Almost always the dramatists and their defenders claimed that any hidden meanings found in their plays would promote virtue and discourage vice.

PROFIT AND DELIGHT

As the evidence assembled by Klein demonstrates, dramatists also justified their art by asserting that plays could produce both profit and delight. In fact, they often claimed that plays could be morally profitable precisely because they held an audience's sustained attention by giving them pleasure. Useful lessons, in other words, could be taught most effectively when the plays teaching them produced satisfaction of one kind or another. This idea was often associated with the ancient Roman writer Horace, and it was extremely influential. It had been endorsed by various Elizabethans, such as Sir Philip Sidney, and it was frequently asserted by dramatists themselves. Thus Udall proclaimed that a play of his mixed "Mirth . . . with virtue in decent comeliness," while the author of *Jack Juggler* suggested that comedy not only offered the "mind comfort" but could also "contain much wisdom, and teach prudent policy." Likewise, the playwright John Lyly, in the prologue to *Campaspe* (ca. 1580–84), claimed to "have mixed mirth with counsel, and discipline with delight," and in various other plays Lyly offered exactly the same rationale for writing dramas.

Comedies, as Klein makes clear, were sometimes justified for providing simple mirth alone, but even mirth was sometimes claimed to have beneficial effects: It relaxed the mind, helped alleviate melancholy, and thus prepared people to return, reinvigorated, to their normal tasks. Claims that plays merely provided mirth were often qualified to suggest that such mirth was innocent, harmless, and modest or that it was simply merry and pleasant rather than sharply or personally satirical.

SATIRE IN PLAYS

Often dramatists denied the presence of satire in their plays, particularly personal or political satire. But they sometimes did so, ironically, partly to encourage audiences to look or listen for precisely that feature. Attacks on specific individuals were sometimes presented in ways allowing for plausible deniability. The same was often true of political or religious satire. Sometimes, however, dramatists claimed (whether honestly or otherwise) that audiences had detected satire and personal mockery when none had really been intended. Plays, after all, were supposed to be read and approved by government censors before they could be performed, but even this requirement did not always prevent controversial mockery from appearing—or seeming to appear—onstage.

Although a few playwrights were willing to confess or imply their satirical motives, they almost always claimed to be satirizing vices in general rather than in particular people. Thus a poet in John Day's play *The Parliament of Bees* (1608–16) defends his satiric talents by arguing that

> satires . . . must lance wide
> The wounds of men's corruptions; ope the side
> Of vice; search deep flesh and rank cores [i.e., hearts].

A poet's ink can better cure some sores
Than surgeon's balsam.

Likewise, Ben Jonson, in the voice of his alter ego Horace in the play *Poetaster* (1601), disclaims any intention to write "lewd verses, such as libels be, / And aimed at persons of good quality." Such libels, Horace asserts, are justly punished. But then he continues:

But if they [i.e., verses] shall be sharp yet modest rhymes,
That spare men's persons and but tax their crimes,
Such shall in open court find current pass,
Were Caesar judge, and with the maker's grace.

Later in the same play, the exemplary Horace contends that

'Tis not the wholesome sharp morality,
Or modest anger of a satiric spirit,
That hurts or wounds the body of the state,
But the sinister application [i.e., interpretation]
Of the malicious, ignorant, and base
Interpreter: who will distort and strain
The general scope and purpose of an author
To his particular and private spleen.

This, indeed, was the current common defense of stage satire: Mockery of general ethical flaws or vices should be permitted, since it promoted public morality. Specific personal attacks, however, should be avoided, since they were likely to be personally motivated and serve no larger public good. Anyone who recognized his own vices depicted onstage should try to overcome them and pursue virtue; anyone who alleged that he was being personally maligned was only calling attention to his genuine flaws and guilty conscience.

Again and again, playwrights claimed that any personal satire discovered in their plays had been imagined by malicious interpreters. Thus Thomas Nashe, in the prologue to *Summer's Last Will and Testament* (ca. 1592), urged those who liked to "wrest a never meant meaning out of everything, applying all things to the present time," to keep their "attention for the common stage; for here are no quips in character for you to read. Vain glosers [i.e., interpreters], gather what you will; Spite, spell backward [to search for hidden meanings] what thou canst." Likewise, John Marston, in his prologue to *The Malcontent* (1602–03), claimed that "To wrest each hurt-

less thought to private sense / Is the foul use of ill-bred impudence." Jonson, in the induction to his play *Bartholomew Fair* (1614), even had a character propose a contract with the play's "hearers and spectators" that

> they neither in themselves conceal, nor suffer by them to be concealed, any state-decipherer [i.e., person searching for political meanings in plays], or politic picklock of the scene, so solemnly ridiculous as to search out who was meant by [various characters, such as] the gingerbread-woman, who by the hobby-horse man, who by the costermonger, nay, who by their wares. Or that will pretend to affirm on his own inspired ignorance, what Mirror of Magistrates is meant by the justice, what great lady by the pig-woman, what concealed statesman by the seller of mouse-traps, and so of all the rest.

Despite such denials, however, personal and political satire was a common feature of many Renaissance English plays. Even the playwrights themselves would sometimes admit this. George Chapman, in his play *All Fools* (ca. 1604), has a character admit that "railing," or personal abuse, had now become "most applausive [i.e., popular]; your best poet is / He that rails grossest." Likewise, Marston, in the prologue to *What You Will* (ca. 1601), noted that "What's out of railing's out of fashion," while Francis Beaumont, in the prologue to his play *The Woman Hater* (ca. 1605–06), denies engaging in "the ordinary and overworn trade of jesting at lords, and courtiers, and citizens." Meanwhile, Lording Barry, in the prologue to *Ram Alley* (ca. 1608), distinguishes between proper general satire and improper, spiteful railing. He claims that his play is "Free from the loathsome stage diseases, / (So overworn, so tired, and stale, / Not satirizing but to rail)." Similarly, an epistle preceding H. Parrot's drama *More the Merrier* (published 1608) asserts that "satiric inveighing at any man's private person" is "a kind of writing which, of late, seems to have [become] very familiar among our poets and players," but Parrot urges his own audience "to seek it elsewhere." This was the standard line: Others might be writing personal or political satire, but the author of the present play was not. Yet the authorities were not always convinced, and various playwrights who denied such satire—including Nashe, Chapman, Jonson, and Marston—were occasionally accused of (and sometimes even arrested and imprisoned for) writing it.

PLAYS ONSTAGE AND ON THE PAGE
Most dramas of Shakespeare's era were written as scripts intended for actual performance. Occasionally, "closet dramas"—intended for reading—were

composed, but these were relatively few, and their authors tended not to be professional playwrights. Most people who wrote plays did so for professional acting companies and earned money for their work. They were paid for their scripts by the companies, which then owned the texts and could do with them whatever they pleased. This included cutting them, altering them, revising them, and reviving them, perhaps in changed versions, whenever they saw fit. Once plays had been paid for, they became the properties of the companies, not the playwrights. Modern copyright did not exist.

Most plays were *not* written with immediate or inevitable publication in mind, and most were never printed. We know about the existence of many more dramas than have actually survived in either manuscript or print. The real financial value of plays lay in their function as scripts for performance. It was in theaters—not in bookstalls—that real money could be made for, and by, the companies. Performance, not printing, was the key to financial success for theater owners, who, like Shakespeare, were often actors or even playwrights themselves.

Sometimes, however, when plays were no longer new or when they had gained sufficient popularity, they would be printed as small, cheap books called "quartos"—usually unbound and not much more than pamphlets in size and appearance. If an author's name on a title page could help sell books (as the names of Shakespeare and some others could), the author's name might be printed. Often, however, quartos were issued anonymously. This was perhaps in part because most plays were co-authored and involved contributions from numerous collaborators. Yet even if no particular author was mentioned, the name of the company that owned the play and had performed it *would* be printed. Published plays thus functioned, in one respect, as advertising for the actors and for the theaters where they performed.

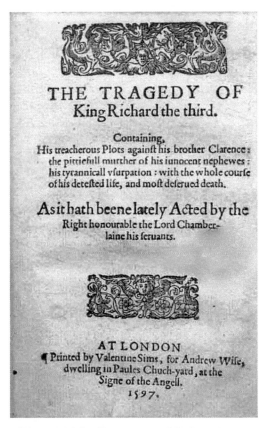

Title page of the first quarto of *Richard III*, without Shakespeare's name, published in 1597.

PLAYS AS WORKS OF LITERATURE

As years passed and London's theatrical scene became increasingly stable and professional, more and more plays *were* printed with their authors' names. Many authors, in fact, began to assume that their plays would be either eventually, or even quickly, published. Some writers—Ben Jonson in particular—thought of their plays almost from the start as literature, intended not only for acting but also, at some point, for serious and thoughtful reading. Jonson was instrumental in helping to turn plays, in the minds of both authors and audiences, into "literature," written with care and meant to be insightfully read, not simply performed. The skill and thought with which many plays were written—particularly Shakespeare's—suggests that many playwrights saw their works as more than simple scripts; they saw them as carefully crafted works of literary art. If nothing else, the actual writing and reading of plays must have given authors like Shakespeare much personal literary pleasure, and there is every reason to think that many members of the theatrical audiences themselves came as much to *hear* and actively *listen* to words as to witness dramatic action.

The best actors were prized as much for their ability to speak eloquently and credibly as for moving their faces or bodies in interesting ways. Even Marston emphasized the importance of words when, in addressing readers of *The Malcontent*, he commented that "one thing afflicts me, to think that scenes invented merely to be spoken should be inforcively published to be read." As time went by, however, Marston's skepticism about the reading of plays was increasingly a minority opinion. In fact, even Marston seems to have been skeptical of the idea of only printing and reading *comedies*, not tragedies. Thus in addressing readers of *The Fawn* (1604–05), he comments that

> If any wonder why I print a comedy, whose life
> rests much in the actor's voice, let such know that it cannot
> avoid publishing. . . . Comedies are writ to be spoken, not read.
> Remember[:] the life of these things consists in action; and for your
> such courteous survey of my pen, I shall present a tragedy to you
> which shall boldly abide the most curious perusal.

READING PLAYS

Shakespeare seemed to have had almost no interest in the printing of his plays. His dramas, according to this common claim, were written to be performed, not published or read. Lukas Erne, however, has recently and forcefully challenged this view, and much suggests that the claim, though widespread, is a great overstatement. If nothing else, Shakespeare wrote to satisfy his own highly sophisticated literary tastes, and he also knew that many audience members—including the most socially influential—were quite literate and could fully appreciate good writing. So could his fellow playwrights and competitors, such as Jonson. These were the people in perhaps the best positions to judge the "literary" merit of his plays, and, when he wrote, he surely had such people at least partially in mind. Shakespeare also knew, of course, that some of his plays might be performed at court, before highly powerful and well-educated people. Finally, he also knew that some of his plays might be published for people to read, whether he wanted them published or not. In his own lifetime, his plays were regularly published, with or without his approval. Indeed, Shakespeare's name on a title page could help sell books. He had every practical incentive, then, to write as well as he could, even if some members of his audiences in the popular theaters could not appreciate all the nuances of his writing.

Many playwrights besides Shakespeare would have known or expected that their plays would be printed and read. Some obviously *wanted* that to happen. Thus the publisher of Edward Sharpham's play *The Fleer* (1606) reports that Sharpham had prepared "an epistle or apological [sic] preamble" intended for readers. Moreover, the publisher himself tells the play's readers that Sharpham felt a "great desire to delight them," hoping that his work, when read, would "be sweet in the palates of [their] minds." Numerous other writers took a hand in preparing their plays to be read. Jonson is the obvious example; Marston is another. Increasingly, however, more and more playwrights knew or even hoped that their dramas would ultimately appear in book form. The fact that some of these early books do not survive has sometimes been taken as evidence that they were "read to death," in the ways that many modern paperbacks are read, resold, reread, and eventually discarded but not often preserved for the ages in prestigious libraries. Yet many playbooks were, in fact, included in numerous private libraries in Shakespeare's era, as Erne has shown. Erne's book is now required reading for anyone who wants to understand how and why plays became "literature," for reading, in Elizabethan and Jacobean England.

THE ORIGINS OF PLAYS

Whether a playwright deliberately wrote with eventual publication in mind, all plays prepared for the public theaters were originally intended for performance. Before it was anything else, a play was a script meant to be acted—a script attractive enough to an acting company that the troupe would want to produce it. Each choice of a play for performance was a calculated financial risk; the company had a vested interest, then, in seeking plays that would be popular and profitable. Scripts that failed onstage would damage a company's finances, while those with enduring appeal could earn profits repeatedly.

The origins of most plays were strikingly similar and have often been described by scholars, including, fairly recently, Grace Iopollo and Scott McMillan. Sometimes a playwright would approach an acting company with an idea for a drama, or sometimes—especially if the playwright's talents were already well known—a company might commission work from a writer. A well-established playwright, like Shakespeare, was probably trusted to generate his own ideas and write most of his scripts alone. Quite often, though, more than one writer was involved in working on most dramas; collaboration was far more common in writing plays in Shakespeare's day than was single authorship. Like the scripts for many television shows or even films today, the final scripts for Renaissance English dramas were often the products of numerous hands. Even when the script was finally deemed complete by the writer or writers, further changes—involving additions or deletions— might be made by the actors as they prepared the work for performance.

In the 1590s, an author might earn as much as £5 to £7 for a play (£20 was the annual salary for the schoolmaster in Shakespeare's hometown). Most plays took roughly six weeks to write. Ben Jonson, however, in the prologue to *Volpone* (1605–06), boasted that "*five weeks fully penned it*" and that it had come "from his own hand, without a co-audjutor [i.e., assistant], / novice, journeyman, or tutor." It had been written, in other words, entirely by Jonson, with no help from anyone. However, when collaborators *were* involved in penning dramas, one writer might be responsible for one section of the play (such as the main plot or the first half), while another might be responsible for another section (such as the subplot or the second half). One writer might do the "serious" parts, and another might handle the comedy.

There was, though, no inevitable or prescribed method for collaborations: Each play was an individual case, although the men who worked on any play were often veteran writers with years of experience as collaborators who would have learned much not only by trial and error but also from one another. Some playwrights contributed to an astonishing number of scripts. Scott McMillan notes that Henry Chettle helped compose 50 plays during five years, while Thomas Dekker contributed to 44 plays in four years. Shakespeare, at the height of his career, usually wrote two plays a year, but he was under far less financial pressure than most playwrights, because he owned a share of any profits made by the company that performed his plays.

He is estimated to have eventually earned £180 to £200 per annum—enough money to finance a very comfortable retirement.

CENSORSHIP OF PLAYS

Once a play had tentatively been accepted for production, it first had to be submitted to the master of the revels, a royal official, for review and approval. He was paid a fee by the company to read the play to ensure that it contained nothing politically or religiously offensive or damaging to the reputations of particular people. Anything deemed too provocative, especially about current events, might well need to be stricken or rewritten. Without approval, a play technically could not be acted. When plays, for some reason or another, were not submitted for approval, or when provocative additions were made by either playwrights or actors after approval had been granted, the possible punishments might be severe. It was to everyone's advantage, then, to be careful, and the number of plays that caused any trouble was small. Playwrights probably had a good sense of what would pass muster and what wouldn't, and so self-censorship (if much censorship were indeed really needed) was probably the most common kind. The livelihood of everyone—playwright, actors, theater owners, and even the censor himself—depended on the generally smooth operation of the system. Iopollo notes that few of the more than 900 surviving plays suggest that playwrights deliberately sought to deceive or provoke the censors.

PREPARING A PLAY FOR PRODUCTION

After the censor had approved a clean and sometimes corrected script, the acting company's "book keeper" could ensure that everything was in order for performance. No individual actor had a copy of the entire script. Making so many handwritten copies would have been impossibly expensive and time consuming. Instead, each actor was given a copy or copies, often on long "rolls" of paper, of the role or roles he would play. Playing more than one role was quite common at this time; plays generally contained more characters than there were actors to play them all if each actor had just one role. Lesser actors, therefore, often played two, three, four or even more parts. Before performance, both playwrights and actors had to be sure to work out all the potential complications. An actor who had just left the stage as one character, for instance, could not easily come back immediately, playing someone else, especially if a time-consuming change of costume was involved.

Actors probably memorized their separate roles in the evenings, after the theaters closed; only when the players came together for rehearsal could they see how their individual parts fit into the whole work. Only then did they begin to get a sense of the play as a total entity. Rehearsal time was brief, because so many different plays were performed in such rapid succession. A different play might be staged each day of the week, with popular plays held over for longer runs. One day an actor might play a tragic hero, and the next day he might play a comic butt. Plays newly written were often staged in rotation with old but newly revived (and sometimes revised) plays, and the minor players who played more than one role in a play might thus be acting 10, 15, 20 or more parts each week. Modern scholars stand in amazement at the memories that must have been required of Elizabethan actors; Scott McMillan calls these skills "one of the unexplained phenomena of human history."

ACTORS AND ACTING

Some actors became both rich and famous. One was Edward Alleyn, who eventually was wealthy enough to endow a noted London college. Alleyn and various other performers—such as Richard Burbage—often played leading parts, with many lines to remember because of their important roles. A play's success was probably determined as much by the skills of these "stars" as by anything else, including the writing. A shoddy performance by a lead actor could hurt even the best-written script, while a superb performance by an especially talented player could lend real interest even to a rather mediocre play. Of course, a play's theatrical success depended greatly on the combined talents of the company as a whole, but there is no doubt that some actors were especially important. This was particularly true of the men who played clowns, fools, or other comic roles. The best of them—such as Richard Tarlton and Will Kemp—became immensely popular and even beloved. Kemp in particular became a kind of comic legend.

Playwrights—especially Shakespeare, who essentially wrote for one company—could often tailor their creation of roles to suit the skills, mannerisms, or even physical appearance of specific actors. A writer such as Shakespeare, who was intimately involved with a relatively stable group of actors over many years (and was also an actor), probably often had particular actors in mind for particular roles as he crafted his plays. Certainly it would have been to the financial advantage of everyone involved to have the best players perform the parts most appropriate to their abilities.

Was there a particular "style" of acting in Shakespeare's day? This has been a much-debated question. Some scholars have suggested that actors during Elizabethan times would seem a bit stiff or formal today, when theatrical standards favor credible, "realistic" performances. Oratory was a greatly respected skill during the Renaissance, and some acting at that time—at least of some roles—may have somewhat resembled delivery of a speech. In addition, some theater historians have argued that gestures tended to be fairly conventional, with particular emotions expressed by familiar or even stereotypical gestures. It is easy, however, to overestimate the differences between acting then and today. In fact, acting styles probably evolved during Shakespeare's lifetime, just as dramatic writing styles evolved as well. Shakespeare's style, at the beginning of his career, was much more formal and predictable than it would later become, and some evidence suggests that acting styles may have become more flexible as well. Contemporary comments suggest that performances by some actors could be a bit wooden and even inept, but there is plenty of other evidence suggesting that seeing a play in an Elizabethan or Jacobean theater could be a powerfully moving experience. In any case, styles of acting probably differed to some degree depending on the theater and company. Declamatory delivery was probably more common in the amphitheaters than in the smaller, more intimate halls.

PROPS AND DÉCOR

The physical characteristics of the two main kinds of theaters have already been described. In the nearly circular outdoor amphitheaters (such as the Globe), which could accommodate perhaps 3,000 people, the stage was elevated about five feet off the ground. It thrust out into the middle of the yard and was therefore surrounded by spectators—either standing or sitting—on three sides. At the rear of the stage were two doors, on opposite sides, designed for entrances and exits. Between them was either a larger opening enclosed by doors or a recessed area, usually covered by a curtain. Above that was a small upper gallery that could sometimes function as a balcony or different kind of upstairs area. It might sometimes house musicians or even spectators. Large props, such as the bed featured at the end of *Othello*, could be kept in the recessed area and sometimes moved out onto the main stage when needed. More often, though (according to Andrew Gurr), even large props were carried onto the stage when needed and then carried off again when no longer necessary. In the smaller indoor "hall" theaters, stages did not reach far out into the enclosed rooms. All the spectators sat, with most sitting in front of the stage and a few even sitting on it.

For the most part, neither complicated props nor elaborate scenery was used. The stage was mainly bare, although Philip Henslowe did list the kinds of props most frequently employed. Gurr reprints this inventory, which begins by mentioning "1 rock, 1 cage, 1 tomb, [and] 1 hell mouth,"

THE SWAN THEATRE IN THE TIME OF SHAKESPEARE
csimile of a Sketch made by John de Witt, a learned Dutchman, during a visit to London in 1596. The Sketch ha
recently been discovered by Dr. Gaedertz, of the Royal Library, Berlin

An 1888 facsimile reproduction of Johannes Dewitt's 1596 drawing of a performance at London's Swan Theatre.

and which continues by listing such other items as lances, bells, a golden scepter, a golden fleece, a bay tree, two different kinds of hatchet, a lion's skin, a bear's skin, and so on. Props and scenery were mainly suggestive rather than elaborately detailed or realistic. Most of the items in Henslowe's list could be carried on and off the stage fairly easily and quickly. Props must have seemed interesting to spectators, but they never came close to being almost more important than the play itself, as is sometimes true today.

Costumes—often once belonging to the wealthy and powerful and either donated or purchased secondhand—were frequently splendid and colorful. They, it seems, were the theaters' main visual attractions. Ross McDonald quotes from a lengthy inventory of costumes compiled by Henslowe. It mentions "A scarlet cloak with 2 broad gold laces with gold buttons of the same down the sides," and it continues by listing "A black velvet cloak, a scarlet cloak laid down with silver lace and silver buttons, a short velvet cap cloak embroidered with gold and gold spangles," and so on. Companies often paid more for costumes than for plays, indicating how highly costumes were valued, in several senses of that word.

Because little time was spent arranging, rearranging, or removing large props, plays could be performed fairly quickly. Pauses between acts were common indoors to allow time for candles to be trimmed. Music was typically played during these necessary breaks, and sometimes even dances were presented. Candles, however, were unnecessary in the amphitheaters, and so plays performed there could move along even more rapidly. In both kinds of theater, a scene ended whenever the stage was briefly empty of actors—usually no more than a few seconds. Many printed plays contained no indications of scene breaks; these have often been added later by editors.

Plays lasted anywhere from two to three hours (usually closer to two), and audience attention would have been much more on the words of the play and much less on spectacular audiovisual effects than is sometimes true today. Effects of sound and sight did sometimes occur: Smoke might appear, small cannons might be fired, artificial thunder might be heard, trumpets might be blown, and occasionally a character would use a trapdoor to arise from below the stage or exit into. Far more rarely, a character might actually descend from the painted roof (the "heavens") that covered part of the rear of the stage outdoors. Mostly, though, the plot and the words—both creations of the writer(s)—were what people paid to watch and hear.

CHANGES AND INNOVATIONS

What were playwrights hoping to achieve, aside from payment and applause, when they sat down to compose? Much depends on the particular years or decades in which they wrote. Fashions in entertainment could change in Shakespeare's era, as often and quickly they do today. Indeed, Thomas Middleton, addressing readers of *The Roaring Girl* (1611), explicitly used the analogy with fashions in clothing: "The fashion of play-making I can properly compare to nothing so naturally as the alteration in apparel; for in the time of the great crop-doublet, your huge bombastic plays, quilted with mighty words to lean purpose, was [sic] only then in fashion." However, "as the doublet fell, neater inventions [in playwriting] began to set up." At present, Middleton continued, "in the time of spruceness [in clothing], our plays follow the niceness of our garments." Thus "single plots, quaint conceits, lecherous jests, dressed up with hanging sleeves" were at present considered most appropriate, while other fashions seemed passé. Numerous other playwrights also compared changes of fashions in writing to changes of fashions in clothes.

As a tradition of writing plays grew up in England (and as it was increasingly preserved in printed plays), more and more playwrights were concerned to make their own new dramas seem fresh or innovative. Many wanted to avoid stale imitations of previous works. Sometimes, however, audiences actually preferred revivals of old plays rather than the challenges posed by anything new or strikingly unfamiliar. Jonson (a highly self-conscious innovator) mocked this tendency when, in *Bartholomew Fair* (1614), a character satirizes audiences who "will swear that *Jeronimo* or *Andronicus* [early works by Kyd and Shakespeare] are the best plays yet." Such outmoded expectations, Jonson ironically proclaims, reveal a judgment that "is constant, and hath stood still these five and twenty or thirty years." Most playwrights seem to have tried to balance what had been done before with what would seem fresh and new. They wrote within established genres but tried to innovate within those broad generic traditions.

USING AND MIXING GENRES

A key decision facing a playwright concerned the particular *kind* of play he would write. Which genre would he use, and which generic patterns would he follow? Would he write a tragedy, a comedy, a history, a pastoral, or some combination of such generic types? Both playwrights and audiences tended to think in terms of distinct genres, as in a character's reference, in Dekker's *The Gull's Hornbook* (1609), to "the middle of [a] play, be it pastoral, comedy, moral, or tragedy," or in a question asked by a character in the opening of Marston's *What You Will* (1601) about the genre of that play: "Is't comedy, tragedy, pastoral, moral, nocturnal, or history?" The term "nocturnal" is probably a joke, but the other genres would have been very familiar to Elizabethans. When they entered a playhouse to see a new drama, they would have had very similar kinds of questions on their minds.

Comedy and tragedy were the main genres and were expected by some people, especially those with classical training, to be kept distinct. But Elizabethan drama quickly became notorious for mixing or juxtaposing different categories in single plays, particularly by adding comic subplots to the more "serious" forms of tragedy or history. Satire, too, became an increasing generic influence, and sometimes the satire was quite stinging and even personal. (Most playwrights, however, were careful to try to conceal obvious attacks on specific individuals.) Many plays had a distinctly satirical edge, and "railing" seems increasingly to have been both popular and profitable, especially in the indoor halls. Yet numerous playwrights claimed that they avoided "railing," and many comic writers, in particular, asserted that they offered simple, harmless "mirth."

STORIES AND TOPICS

As David Klein notes, the biblical and religious topics that had provided popular material for plays in the Middle Ages became far less prominent in theaters of the English Renaissance. Probably this change resulted mainly from the Reformation, which made religious topics suddenly controversial, particularly in Protestant nations, such as England, with strong Catholic histories and substantial Catholic minorities. Religious topics were therefore especially sensitive and potentially dangerous matters during Shakespeare's lifetime, and so it is not surprising that explicitly religious plays were far less common then than they had been a century earlier.

The topics that *could* be dealt with onstage were still plentiful. Klein quotes a lengthy catalog of potential topics cited by playwright Robert Wilson in his play *Three Ladies of London* (1581), in which Wilson details all the common subjects he will deliberately avoid: "We do not show of warlike fight, as sword and shield to shake; / We speak not of the powers divine, nor yet of furious sprites; / . . . We do not here present to you the thresher with his flail; / We do not here present to you the milkmaid with her pail," and so on. A similar list was presented roughly two decades later by Thomas Tomkis in the prologue to *Lingua*, which promises that "Our muse describes no lover's passion, / No wretched father, no unthrifty son, / No craven subtle whore, or shameless bawd, / No stubborn clown, or daring parasite, / No lying servant, or bold sycophant." By rejecting all these common topics, however, Tomkis indicates the kinds of plots and characters that regularly *did* appear in contemporary plays.

Meanwhile, playwright Thomas Heywood conveniently listed the many kinds of sources dramatists could and did consult in their search for stage-worthy material:

> . . . no history
> We have left unrifled; our pens have been dipped
> As well in opening each hid manuscript
> As tracts more vulgar, whether read or sung,
> In our domestic or more foreign tongue . . . .
> Nay, 'tis known
> That when our [historical] chronicles have barren grown
> Of story, we have all invention stretched . . .

Works by ancient Greeks and especially ancient Roman writers provided copious material, but so, as Heywood suggests, did English histories and continental history and fiction. Contemporary personalities and events, both in England and abroad, provided subjects for numerous plays, and contemporary London itself soon became the setting of many dramas. In a period when people generally believed that "All the world's a stage, / And all the men and women merely players" (Shakespeare, *As You Like It*, 2.7.139–40), almost any person, episode, or idea might someday be featured in a drama.

THE PLOT

Once a story or stories—whether historical or fictional—had been selected, the next crucial step was to shape such raw material into a coherent plot, often involving a subplot as well. It was in the construction of such plots that artistic craftsmanship was crucially shown, and dramatists were well aware that their plays might fail if their plots seemed seriously defective. Thus John Fletcher, in a play coauthored with Francis Beaumont and titled *The Captain* (1612–13), cleverly calls attention to a somewhat hasty marriage in his own drama by having a character say, "If a marriage should be thus stubber'd up in a play, ere almost / Anybody had taken notice you were in love, the spectators / Would take it to be but ridiculous." Many audience members, it seems, expected plot developments to be well integrated and well prepared for. Incidents that seemed abruptly or inexplicably inserted were very likely to be criticized, especially if they appeared in the final act. Ideally, all elements of a plot should work together and contribute to a drama's whole effectiveness, yet none should seem contrived or implausible. This ideal of total integration is implied, for example, when a character in Cyril Tourneur's *The Atheist's Tragedy* (published in 1611) describes a "most judicious murder" by praising its "plot":

Not any circumstance
That stood within the reach of the design,
Of persons, dispositions, matter, time, or place,
But by this brain of mine was made
An instrumental help; yet nothing from
The induction to the accomplishment seemed forced,
Or done o' purpose, but by accident.

In other words, every incident seemed credible and natural ("by accident") rather than obviously contrived, even though the plot resulted from careful design and thoughtful skill.

This same ideal of careful integration is also implied in George Chapman's *The Gentleman Usher* (ca. 1602–04), in which one character praises a "show" created by another by saying, "'Twas the best fashion'd and well-ordered thing / That ever eye beheld . . . . / . . . every part / Concurring to one commendable end." Likewise, the unknown author of *Alphonsus, Emperor of Germany* (1594) promised readers that "The design is high, the contrivance subtle," while John Lyly, in the prologue to *Midas* (1589) apologizes for the work's possible lack of unity by announcing that "If we present a mingle-mangle, our fault is to be excused, because the whole world is become a hodge-podge."

As Klein notes, sometimes these ideals of careful construction and unity were presented in classical terms, as when Thomas Heywood, in his *An Apology for Actors*, describes the proper structure of a comedy by saying that such a work should consist of "the *Prologue*, that is, the preface; the *Protasis*, that is, the proposition, which includes the first act, and presents the actors; the *Epitasis*, which is the business and body of the comedy; the last, the *Catastrophe*, and conclusion."

Some audience members apparently expected sophisticated and complex plots. John Fletcher, in the prologue to *The Woman's Prize* (1605), entreats "angry men" not to anticipate "the mazes of a subtle plot," just as he likewise uses the prologue to *The Chances* (1613) to ask the audience not to "Expect strange turns and windings in the plot." Indeed, there seems to have been wide agreement that undue complexity and length should be avoided, especially if the

Title page of a 1615 edition of Thomas Kyd's *The Spanish Tragedie* (Printed by W. White).

play were otherwise flawed to begin with. The main character of Kyd's *The Spanish Tragedy* (1587), for example, promises (concerning a play he plans to write) that "all shall be concluded in one scene, / For there's no pleasure ta'en in tediousness." Similarly, John Lyly, in the epilogue to his play *Sapho and Phao* (1584), apologized for any "wearisome travail" in the unfolding of the plot, telling audience members that they "must impute [any such flaw] to the necessity of the history" (i.e., source of the plot). Meanwhile, a character in John Webster's *The Devil's Law Case* (1610) asks, "are not bad plays / The worse for their length?" Defensiveness about overly long plays can be found again and again in prologues and epilogues from this period.

Conclusions of plays seem to have been considered especially important. Thus the chorus in the anonymously written play *Thomas Lord Cromwell* (1600) asks the audience to "Pardon the errors . . . already past, / And live in hope the best doth come at last," while a character in Webster's *The Devil's Law Case* urges that the "last act" should be "the best in the play." The ending of a play was expected to be memorable, effective, and well integrated with the rest of the plot. Conclusions that seemed obviously contrived and unprepared for were typically condemned. The best Elizabethan playwrights seem to have strongly sensed the need for artistry and skill in constructing their plots.

CHARACTERS AND CHARACTERIZATION

Once a genre or genres had been chosen and a general plot devised, appropriate characters had to be created. In accordance with a principle known as *decorum*, it was particularly important that a character should speak credibly. If he were an old man, he should speak as old men tended to do; if he were a boy, he should not sound like an old man. An aristocratic character would speak in one way; a character from the very lowest classes would not speak like an aristocrat. This tendency to think of characters partly as character *types* not only reflected common assumptions about human psychology but also reflected the practical conditions of writing for theater. Most playwrights simply had too little time to make characters highly individualized, with extremely complex "personalities." Shakespeare's Hamlet, in other words, was the exception, not the rule.

This habit of treating characters somewhat stereotypically can be seen at least as early as Richard Edwards's play *Damon and Pythias* (1564), where the prologue notes the playwright's obligation "to frame each person so, / That by his common talk you may his nature know: / A royster [i.e., ruffian] ought not preach: that were too strange to hear." According to Edwards, "The old man is sober, the young man rash, the lover triumphing in joys; / The matron grave, the harlot wild and full of wanton toys." All of a drama's characters should speak in appropriate ways. According to George Whetstone, in the dedication to his 1578 play *Promos and Cassandra*, the use of "one order of speech for all persons" was "a gross indecorum," for just as "a crow will counterfeit ill the nightingale's sweet voice: even so, affected speech doth misbecome a clown." Characters in plays were sometimes even identified simply by their roles ("king," "prince," "clown," "vice," etc.) rather than by particular names, and the tendency to think of people onstage as largely stereotypical was a holdover from medieval and even classical drama.

Characters, according to Whetstone and many others, should not only speak in appropriate ways but should also behave appropriately as well: "kindly grave old men should instruct; young men should show the imperfections of youth; strumpets should be lascivious; boys unhappy; and clowns should be disorderly." This principle of decorum was so important to Ben Jonson that he complained three different times, during one set of personal conversations, that even the best authors had sometimes failed to follow it. Sir Philip Sidney, Jonson told a friend, "did not keep decorum in making everyone speak as well as himself." Later, Jonson once again objected that Giovanni Guarini, an influential Italian author, "in his *Pastor Fido,* kept not decorum, in making shepherds speak as well as himself could." Finally, Jonson summed up his feelings once more by saying that "Lucan [an important Roman writer], Sidney, [and] Guarini make every man speak as well as themselves, forgetting decorum." Of course, few playwrights were as concerned to follow strict literary rules as Jonson was, but most did tend to present characters in fairly stereotypical terms, as dramatists have tended to do throughout history.

STYLE AND SPEECH: AVOIDING "FUSTIAN" AND "INKHORN" TERMS

For the Elizabethans even more than for most dramatists, making plays involved close attention to styles of language and kinds of speech. Once a genre had been selected, and once a plot had been chosen that seemed appropriate to that genre, and once characters had been selected to fit that plot, those characters had to be given appropriate styles of speaking. Yet Elizabethan dramatists were also concerned with—and judged by—the overall styles of particular plays. In general, a tragedy would have a different kind of style (loftier, more poetic, more thoughtful and profound) than a comedy. Likewise, a comedy would have a style lighter, breezier, more mundane, and more facetious than that of a tragedy. Comic subplots in tragedies were often written in prose to distinguish them in tone and flavor from the heightened verse surrounding them. A playwright's talent was measured not only by the appropriateness of the speeches of individual characters but also by the broader appeal of an entire play's "style." More than half the pleasure of attending an Elizabethan drama must have been the simple pleasure of listening to the poet's skillful use of words.

This need for stylistic talent is a recurring theme in contemporary comments about plays, especially in prologues and epilogues. Lack of such talent was frequently satirized, sometimes viciously. Old-fashioned language, for example, was often mocked, as when a character in the anonymously written, undated play *Wily Beguiled* ridicules what he calls "patch-panel stuff, old gallimaufries and cotton-candle eloquence." Comically furious, he commands the character who uses such phrasing, "out, you bawling bandog fox-fired slave! you dried stockfish you, out of my sight!" Likewise, a character in the prologue to John Day's *The Isle of Gulls* (1606) vigorously rejects what he calls "mere fustian" (i.e., inflated, turgid, or pompous language), saying, "I had rather hear two good bawdy jests than a whole play of such tear-cat thunderclaps." Much of this later mockery of "fustian" was aimed at the kind of lofty, soaring style Marlowe promised in the prologue to *Tamburlaine the Great* (Part I; 1587). There Marlowe had vowed, "you shall hear the Scythian Tamburlaine / Threat'ning the world with high astounding terms."

Such language, thrilling to those who first heard it, later came to seem—at least to many playwrights—enormously overblown, unsubtle, and unsophisticated. Indeed, language of this sort was already being rejected even before Marlowe made it so famous and influential. The author of an undated play called *Fedele and Fortunio*, for instance, promises that he will use "no words of thundering state," having "clipped his wings, to keep a meaner gait." As Elizabethan drama developed, more and more writers sought a style that would not seem ridiculously exaggerated or artificial. Besides being wary of "fustian," they also increasingly began to reject language that seemed more the product of the study than the street. Artificially ornate phrasing, often derived from scholarly reading and often having little contact with "real" speech, was sometimes savagely mocked. Such "inkhorn words," as they are called in the undated play *The Birth of Hercules*, were gleefully satirized. Perhaps the most memorable example of such mockery occurs in Jonson's *Poetaster* (1601), where a poet modeled on Jonson gives a poet modeled on Marston a pill to make him vomit forth many of his favorite "inkhorn" terms, such as *glibbery, lubrical, magnificate, barmy froth, turgidous, ventositous, oblatrant, furibund,* and *prorumped.* By satirizing his rival's inflated rhetoric, Jonson makes Marston look ludicrous and absurd.

PRAISE OF "WIT"

One quality of style that apparently did impress many Elizabethan playwrights and their audiences was "wit." This word once had much broader meanings than it has today; it was often associated with reason, intellect, and the creativity (or "invention") that resulted in careful craftsmanship and artistic skill. When the word arises within and about Elizabethan plays, it often suggests what the *Oxford English Dictionary* calls "quickness of intellect or liveliness of fancy, with capacity of apt expression." The word *apt* once again suggests *decorum*: A play's words must be appropriate to the play's interlinked genre, plot, and characters. Playwrights seem to have been admired most when they could make their language seem fitting to every other aspect of a work.

Beaumont and Fletcher, for instance, promised audiences of *The Woman's Prize* (1605) a

> comedy, in which
> A rivulet of pure wit flows, strong and rich
> In fancy, language, and all parts that may
> Add grace and ornament to a merry play.

Likewise, when Fletcher's *The Faithful Shepherdess* (1608) initially failed theatrically, his friend Beaumont wrote a poem (printed in the first edition) asking,

> Why should the man, whose wit ne'r had a stain,
> Upon the public stage present his vein,
> And make a thousand men in judgment sit,
> To call in question his undoubted wit . . .

Later, Fletcher praised this very play itself for having been with "so much wit and Art adorned," while Beaumont, in the epilogue to his own later drama *Love's Cure* (1619), anticipated criticisms of various kinds, including especially a lack of wit and other failures of style. Some members of the audience, he feared, would criticize the play because it "wanted wit," because its "language [was] low," and because "very few scenes were writ / With spirit and life." Meanwhile, the publisher of the first collected edition of John Lyly's plays (1632) commended them as "rare monuments of wit" and said of Lyly himself that "few (or none) of our poets now are such witty companions." *Wit*, then, could be simultaneously a quality of the poet's mind, an important feature of his style, and even a synonym for the word *poet* itself.

MAKING PLAYS AND EARNING PRAISE

In whatever ways wit was defined, it was just one of many qualities Elizabethan playwrights strove for in their writings and for which they were sometimes praised. Thus Beaumont, in the prologue to his wonderfully entertaining play *The Knight of the Burning Pestle* (1607), asserts that his "intent was at this time to move inward delight, not outward lightness; and to breed (if it might be) soft smiling, not loud laughing, knowing it (to the wise) to be a great pleasure to hear counsel mixed with wit." Meanwhile, Marston, in the prologue to *Antonio and Mellida* (1599), expresses a wish that his muse might possess

> those abstruse and sinewy faculties,
> That with a strain of fresh invention

She might press out the rarity of art,
The purest elixed juice of rich conceit [i.e., conception],
In your attentive ears; that with the lip
Of gracious elocution, we might drink
A sound carouse unto your health of wit.

Similarly lofty ambitions are announced in the prologue to *If It Be Not Good, the Devil Is in It* (1611), where Thomas Dekker proclaims that a talented playwright can tie the listener's

> ear (with golden chains) to his melody:
> Can draw with Adamantine Pen even creatures
> Forged out of th' hammer, on tiptoe, to reach up,
> And (from rare silence) clap their brawny hands,
> T' applaud what their charmed soul scarce understands.
> That Man give me whose breast filled by the muses
> With raptures into a second them infuses:
> Can give an actor sorrow, rage, joy, passion,
> Whilst he again (by self-same agitation)
> Commands the hearers, sometimes drawing out tears,
> Then smiles, and fills them both with hopes and fears.

Sometimes the expressed intentions of playwrights were far less ambitious than this, particularly in comedies. Middleton's *The Widow*, for instance, contains a brief prologue professing that

> A sport, only for Christmas, is the play
> This hour presents t'you; to make you merry,
> Is all th'ambition 't has; and fullest aim
> Bent at your smiles, to win itself a name:
> And if your edge be not quite taken off,
> Wearied with sports, I hope 'twill make you laugh.

Similarly modest was the anonymous author of *Liberality and Prodigality* (1601), who began his play by downplaying the significance of his work, professing that

> this we bring, is but to serve the time,
> A poor device, to pass the day withal:
> To loftier points of skill we dare not clime,
> Lest perking over-high, with shame we fall.

Such as doth best beseem such as we be,
Such we present, and crave your courtesy.

Yet whatever their stated aims—whether lofty or low—playwrights knew that ultimately the commercial success or failure of their works depended on audience response, and so it is not surprising that numerous plays from this period either begin or end (or both) by asking attendees to be generous and tolerant.

APPEALING TO VARIOUS TASTES

Such generosity was needed, because the qualities of writing that people might either admire or condemn varied greatly. This issue is comically discussed at length in the opening of John Day's play *The Isle of Gulls* (1606), where different characters express different preferences for such various stylistic traits as "bawdry," "railing," "invectives," and "scurrile jests," while another character says that he most admires "stately-penned histories." Day is obviously joking about the sheer variety of audience desires, a variety that made any particular audience quite hard to please. As one character puts it, any poet can be criticized for practically any reason: If a poet writes "mirth,"

'tis [condemned as] ribaldry, and mean,
Scorned of chaste ears. If he compose a scene
Of high-writ poesy, fitting a true stage,
'Tis counted fustian: If poetic rage
Strike at abuse, or ope the vein of sin,
He is straight inform'd against for libeling.
Neither quick mirth, invective, nor high state
Can content all: such is the boundless hate
Of a confused audience.

Many similar comments by playwrights can be cited. Thus the prologue to Middleton's play *No Wit, No Help Like a Woman* (1613) begins by asking,

How is't possible to suffice [i.e., satisfy]
So many ears, so many eyes?
Some in wit, some in shows
Take delight, and some in clothes;
Some for mirth they chiefly come,
Some for passion, for both some;
Some for lascivious meetings, that's their arrant;
Some to detract, and ignorance their warrant.

How is't possible to please
Opinion tos'd in such wild seas!

Likewise, the author of *Liberality and Prodigality* (1601) notes that

The proverb is, How many men, so many minds.
Which maketh proof how hard a thing it is
Of sundry minds to please the sundry kinds.
In which respect, I have inferred this:
    That where men's minds appear so different,
    No play, no part, can all alike content.

The grave divine [i.e., minister] calls for divinity;
The civil student, for philosophy:
The courtier craves some rare sound history:
The baser sort [yearn] for knacks of pleasantry.
    So every sort desireth specially,
    What thing may best content his fantasy.

The prologue to John Fletcher's *The Captain* (1612) conceded that "all men's eyes, ears, faiths, and judgments, are not of one size," and many playwrights would have agreed with George Chapman's concession, in the epilogue to *All Fools* (1612), which admitted that "Sometimes feasts please the cooks and not the guests."

THE LACK OF VARIOUS TASTES

Ironically, while playwrights often complained that audience tastes were too diverse, sometimes audiences were also accused of lacking independent tastes at all. Thus a character early in John Day's *The Isle of Gulls* (1606) mocks an audience for behaving "like a flock of sheep, that one cannot leap over a hedge, but all the rest will follow." Another character earlier claims that it is now "grown into a custom at plays [that] if any one rise (especially of any fashionable sort) about what serious business soever, the rest, thinking it in dislike of the play, though he never thinks it, cry 'mew,' 'by Jesus: vile!' and leave the poor heartless children [i.e., heartbroken boy actors] to speak their Epilogue to the empty seats."

When Fletcher's *The Faithful Shepherdess* (1608) at first failed in the theater, his friend Beaumont attacked the initial audience (and many audiences in general) by claiming in the printed edition that

Among the rout [i.e., the entire audience] there is not one that hath
In his own censure [i.e., opinion] an explicit faith;

One company [i.e., group], knowing they judgment lack,
Ground their belief on the next man in black;
Others, on him that makes signs, and is mute;
Some like as he does in the fairest suit;
He [reacts] as his mistress doth, and she by chance;
Nor want there those who, as the boy doth dance
Between the acts, will censure the whole play,
Some if the wax-lights be not new that day;
But multitudes there are whose judgment goes
Headlong according to the actors' clothes.

Audiences, then, could displease playwrights by being either too diverse or too uniform.

WRITING FOR THE IDEAL AUDIENCE: IMAGINATION

What kinds of auditors did playwrights desire? If the evidence of numerous prologues and epilogues is any indication, the basic traits they sought were sympathy, kindness, and forgiveness. If a play didn't please, the playwrights and actors at least hoped that their lapses would be pardoned or not strongly censured. The anonymous author of the undated *Every Woman in Her Humor*, for instance, expresses an early wish that the play's audience will "hear with patience, judge with lenity, and correct with smiles." The prologue to the anonymously written play *The Merry Devil of Edmonton* (1602) begins by asking the audience for "your silence and attention, worthy friends" and concludes by asking for their "patience." The prologue to Robert Daborne's *A Christian Turn'd Turk* (1612) concludes by announcing that "Our ship's afloat; we fear nor rocks nor sands, / Knowing we are environed with your helping [i.e., applauding] hands."

This emphasis on the inevitable dependence of the playwright and players on the good will of the audience often takes the form of suggesting that no play can succeed unless an audience, using its collective imagination, assists in bringing it to life. Thus the prologue to John Day's *The Travails of Three English Brothers* (1607) announces that "Our scene lies speechless, active, but yet dumb: / Till your expressing thoughts give it a tongue." Later in the same play, a character asks Day's audience to

Imagine now the gentle breath of heaven
Hath on the liquid high-way of the waves
Conveyed him [another character] many thousand leagues from us.
Think you have seen him sail by many lands,
And now at last arrived in Persia,

Within the confines of the great Sophy;
Think you have heard his courteous salute
Speak in a peal of shot, the like, till now
Ne're heard at Casbin, which town's governor,
Doth kindly entertain our English knight—

Playwrights working in theaters without elaborate props or astounding special effects often had to appeal to the imaginations of their audiences. In this sense, Elizabethan plays were more like radio dramas than like movies, television shows, or even modern plays: Engaging the imaginations of audiences was crucial to the success of many Renaissance dramas. Thus Dekker, in the prologue to his play *Old Fortunatus* (1596), has a chorus express the hope that among the audience,

some will deign [i.e., be willing] to smile, where all might frown:
And for [i.e., because] this small circumference [i.e., the theater] must
    stand
For the imagin'd surface of much land
Of many kingdoms, and since many a mile
Should here be measured out: our muse entreats
Your thoughts to help poor art, and to allow [i.e., permit]
That I may serve as Chorus to her scenes.
She begs your pardon, for she'll send me forth
Not when the laws of poesy do call,
But as the story needs; your gracious eye
Gives life to Fortunatus' history

It seems safe to say that almost all Elizabethan playwrights realized that they depended on the good will and cooperative imaginations of their audiences, as even Shakespeare himself concedes again and again in various plays, particularly in the choruses of *Henry V.* Not only playwrights but also actors had to rely, crucially, on the play's words if they hoped to succeed, and it was thanks in large part because of those words that audiences were able to participate imaginatively in the full experience of the plays.

WRITING FOR THE IDEAL AUDIENCE: JUDGMENT

Just as important to the playwrights and actors as the imaginative participation of audiences was the audience's exercise of informed, intelligent judgment. The complaint that some audiences judged without comprehending recurs often in prologues and epilogues, and so does the desire for well-informed and thoughtful judgment. Ben Jonson was particularly emphatic in complaining against audiences who felt entitled to judge plays merely for paying the price of admission. In his defense of the failed first performances of Fletcher's *The Faithful Shepherdess* (1608), for instance, Jonson sarcastically described to Fletcher how

> The wise, and many headed bench, that sits
> Upon the life and death of plays and wits
> (Compos'd of gamester, captain, knight, knights man,
> Lady, or pucell [i.e., whore], that wears mask or fan,
> Velvet, or taffata cap, rank'd in the dark
> With the shop's foreman, or some such brave spark,
> That may judge for his six-pence) had, before
> They saw it half, damn'd thy whole play, and more.

Although this passage might seem to reflect strong social prejudices, it actually doesn't: Jonson condemns knights and ladies as quickly as he condemns the shop's foreman, and socially prominent people are far more numerous in his list than anyone of low social standing. (Even the one worker mentioned is a foreman, not a laborer.) What bothers Jonson, then, is not social inferiority but rather a lack of informed understanding and intelligent judgment. Lack of social status is not the problem; lack of wisdom is.

Many playwrights shared Jonson's emphasis on the virtues of informed judgment rather than hasty, impulsive reactions. Marston, for instance, in the prologue to *The Dutch Courtesan* (1605), claimed that although there would be "some few . . . of purpose here [in the theater] to tax and scout [i.e. to attack and criticize]," they should know that firm art cannot fear

> Vain rage: only the highest grace we pray
> Is, you'll not tax, until you judge our play.
> Think and then speak: 'tis rashness and not wit
> To speak what is in passion and not judgment fit.

Playwrights often claimed that they really desired not to please everyone (since doing so would be impossible) but to please the most thoughtful and discerning. Thus Robert Daborne, in the epilogue to *A Christian Turn'd Turk* (1612), asserts that anyone

> Who writes and thinks to please the general taste,
> Where eyes and ears are fed, shall find he hath placed

His work with the fond [i.e., foolish] painter, who did mend
So long that, striving to please others, [he] gave no end
To his own labors; for us, . . . if [we can] not [please] all,
We know we have pleased some whose judgments fall
Beyond the common rank, to whom we humbly yield
Ourselves and labors.

It was, in other words, not so much the ignorant or the masses whose approval many playwrights sought but rather the appreciation of those capable of judging their work wisely. Thus John Mason, in the prologue to *The Turk* (1607), claimed to seek the approval of those capable of "serious and impartial hearing, / Sound sense, quick [i.e., perceptive] sight and judgment never erring." He wanted not so much to impress the many but rather to "ravish choicest ears."

Of course, playwrights were not naïve. They knew that one main obligation—indeed, perhaps their chief obligation—was to help make money for the companies that staged their plays. They also knew that the tastes of many members of their audiences were not uniformly high. Thus Dekker, in the prologue to *If It Be Not Good, the Devil Is in It* (1611), contends that it is

with poets now, as 'tis with nations:
Th'ill-favoredst vices are the bravest [i.e., most attractive] fashions.
A play whose rudeness Indians would abhor,
If't fill a house with fish-wives rare, they all roar [in approval].
It is not praise is sought for now but pence,
Though dropped from greasy-apron audience.

Dekker hopes that any playwright who demeans himself (and his art form) by seeking such approval will be

Clapped . . . with thunder that plucks bays [i.e., writes poetry]
With such foul hands and with squint eyes does gaze
On Pallas's [i.e., the goddess of wisdom] shield; not caring (so he gains)
A crammed third day, what[ever] filth drops from his brains.

A playwright whose drama pleased audiences enough to be held over for a third day received a bonus, and so Dekker here mocks any dramatists who write mainly for money. He implies that there were many, and he also implies that it was those dramatists who appealed to the lowest common denominator who profited most in the theaters.

THE ACHIEVEMENT OF ELIZABETHAN DRAMA

Although Dekker satirizes playwrights and audiences alike, and although much similar satire could easily be quoted, the astonishing thing about early modern drama is in fact how *good* it is. Much of it is very well written, and plenty of evidence suggests that much of it appealed to many of the most insightful and thoughtful minds of the period. The players and playwrights were often welcomed at court; they visited the universities and were well received in many provincial towns; and although many very literate people not only wrote for the theaters, many more such people praised their writing in the highest terms. Tributes to Shakespeare and Jonson began to be written well before either man had died, and the same was true of many other Elizabethan dramatists. The flood of praise has only risen over the centuries, and the value of plays as literature, not simply as works for theater, was quickly recognized during the dramatists' own times. More and more plays began to be printed, and one reason that more printed plays do not survive may be that they were literally read to pieces. The flimsy quarto pamphlets in which most of them were first published were the paperbacks of their day—cheap, popular, but not particularly durable. Even so, many private libraries of the period contained plays, and many intelligent people read them and praised them.

Perhaps the most remarkable fact about the writing done for the public theaters is that it became so good so quickly. No long tradition of such writing existed in England, and the earliest plays by the early Elizabethans do often seem awkward and amateurish. They were frequently criticized for such flaws mere decades after they were written. Even works by Marlowe, the first of the truly great Elizabethan dramatists, quickly came to seem old-fashioned, and the same was especially true of Thomas Kyd's *The Spanish Tragedy* (1587), a highly influential play that remained popular but was soon often mocked by later dramatists. Within a few brief decades, the new generation of playwrights, of whom Shakespeare and Jonson were only the most famous, had managed to produce a kind of literature quickly recognized as some of the best English writing of any kind ever done. Eventually the plays of Shakespeare, at least, would be widely regarded as some of the best writing ever done in human history.

Yet the plays of Shakespeare and his contemporaries were rooted in a recent tradition that was, at best, only decades old. Of course, Elizabethan dramatists drew on classic works by the Greeks and Romans (especially the Romans), and they also drew on more recent literature from continental

Europe. Even so, the amount and general quality of their own dramas often seem astonishing, and the plays that survive are just a fragment of those that were written. Shakespeare's dramas were preserved in a handsome folio edition published nine years after his death (only the second such volume devoted to a contemporary dramatist, Jonson's being the first). The folio's publication suggests how quickly his plays were recognized as valuable literature worthy to be read and reread, not simply acted. Shakespeare set a high literary standard for the plays of his day, and, as perhaps the most successful and most influential dramatist of his time, he inevitably helped shape a broader literary culture. The best of his fellow playwrights knew, when they wrote, that their works would inevitably be compared to his and judged accordingly. Jonson, of course, was yet another influential colleague and competitor, and so were several others. A good case can be made that when the Elizabethan playwrights composed their works, they had the works of their friends and rivals in mind as much as anything else. Inevitably, they wrote to please audiences, but surely they also wrote to win the respect and admiration of the best of their fellow dramatists. In this case, a high tide lifted many boats, and the presence of a writer as talented as Shakespeare must have helped inspire his colleagues and competitors to try to do their own best work.

A GALLERY OF
SHAKESPEARE'S CONTEMPORARIES

Although Shakespeare is the best-known writer of his era, and perhaps of any era, he was preceded and surrounded by an unusually talented group of contemporaries, some of whom he knew well and some of whom he knew mainly by reputation. Some of these authors demonstratively influenced his writings; others were influenced by his works; and in some cases the influence was mutual. Shakespeare was hardly an isolated genius; instead, he was part of a larger, vibrant literary milieu that brought literature to a higher level of achievement than ever before in English history. Indeed, few eras in British literature have ever had quite as much impact as the era of Shakespeare and his fellow Elizabethans.

SIR PHILIP SIDNEY

Partly because of his life but also partly because of his writings, Sir Philip Sidney (1554–86) was exceptionally influential. Born into a prominent family (his father served several times as lord deputy of Ireland; his mother was the sister of one of Queen Elizabeth's favorites), Sidney seemed destined for an eminent role in politics or society. As a youth he traveled widely in Europe during one of the so-called "Grand Tours" designed to give likely future leaders extended firsthand exposure to people and life on the Continent. While traveling, he met—and often highly impressed—many leading intellectual, religious, and political figures of his time. His own talents were evident very early. A deeply committed Protestant, on his return to England he joined the faction at court trying to move Elizabeth toward militant Protestantism. She, however, was more usually cautious about religion and foreign policy, and when Sidney overstepped bounds by opposing her potential marriage to a foreign Catholic, she temporarily banished him from her presence.

During this enforced absence, Sidney composed *The Arcadia*, a huge prose romance and one of his most influential works. Subsequent and equally influential works included *Astrophil and Stella* (an early major sonnet sequence illustrating the follies of passion) and the *Apology for Poetry*. Sidney was also important as a patron of other writers and as an exemplar of the proper role of an Elizabethan author. He would have claimed (rightly) that all his writings

A 1576 portrait of the poet and courtier Sir Philip Sidney, by an unknown artist.

were designed to promote Christian ethics. Indeed, the poet's obligation to promote virtue by writing well is the main argument of the *Apology*. There Sidney defines poetry as "an art of *imitation* . . . that is to say, a representing, counterfeiting, or figuring forth to speak metaphorically. [It is a] speaking picture, with this end: to teach and delight." Whenever Sidney writes *about* poetry he also writes with the vividness of a true poet, especially when he emphasizes the poet's power to command attention through memorable phrasing. Thus he writes that "he [i.e., the poet] cometh unto you with a tale which holdeth children from play and old men from the chimney corner." It is precisely the poet's ability to command attention through skilled use of language that makes him the ideal figure to teach virtue by giving pleasure.

Sidney's devotion to Protestant Christianity, and his contempt for Catholic Spain, led him to volunteer for military service in the Netherlands, where the Spanish were attempting to impose their power and religion on Dutch Protestants. Unfortunately, Sidney was wounded by a musket ball shot into his thigh. He died nearly a month later, after enduring enormous pain. Although only 32, he had lived an extraordinarily rich and accomplished life, especially as a writer. His public funeral was extremely elaborate and memorable. The English clearly knew that one of their finest, a young man of exceptional talent and great potential, had been lost. Sidney's works and personal example inspired numerous later writers, including many in his own extended family, especially his beloved sister, Mary, the Countess of Pembroke. (With her he had worked on metrical translations of the biblical psalms.) Later Sidneys would become renowned as patrons and even as writers themselves. Sidney had shown what it could mean to be a worthy Elizabethan author.

JOHN LYLY

John Lyly (1554?–1606) was the grandson of William Lily, a highly influential writer about grammar and headmaster at St. Paul's school in London. An uncle, meanwhile, was employed as secretary by a prominent churchman during the reign of Henry VIII. Lyly, then, came naturally by his talent for writing and his interest in pursuing favor with the powerful. After studying at Oxford, he moved to London in approximately 1576, where he soon became famous for writing a prose romance titled *Euphues: The Anatomy of Wit*, a work of fiction that deals with such topics as love and religion but is far more important for its highly elaborate style than for its complicated plot. Although the title character, a young man who ignores good counsel, grows in wisdom after making various mistakes, it is Lyly's ornate phrasing that became greatly influential.

"Euphuism" is known for strongly emphasizing (perhaps overemphasizing) balanced, alliterative syntax and for stressing paradoxes and opposites. Lyly introduces Euphues, for instance, with a sentence saying that it was uncertain "whether he were more bound to Nature for the lineaments of his person, or to Fortune for the increase of his possessions." Later he is said to be a person "of wit more than wealth, and yet of more wealth than wisdom," and later still Lyly writes that "As therefore the sweetest rose hath his prickle, the finest velvet his brack [i.e, break], the fairest flower his bran [i.e., husk] so the sharpest wit hath his wanton will, and the holiest head his wicked way." This sentence is entirely typical not only in its structure but in its blatantly moral emphasis. Lyly demonstrates (indeed, helped create) the Elizabethan penchant for playing with language while claiming to promote moral behavior. *Euphues* proved so popular that he quickly wrote a similar sequel.

As a playwright, Lyly was known especially for comedies written for boys and performed indoors and also at court. Among his best-known plays were *Campaspe* (1580), *Sapho and Phao* (1584), *Gallathea* (1584), and *Endimion* (1588). In typical Renaissance fashion, these are highly influenced by classical precedent. They emphasize witty dialogue and elaborate speeches, and their announced motives are typically moral. Thus a prologue to *Campaspe* (which was performed both in the public hall and before the queen) promises that "We have mixed mirth with counsel, and discipline with delight." Similarly, a prologue to *Sapho and Phao* reminds the public audience that to wise people, "it is as great a pleasure to hear counsel mixed with wit" as it is "to the foolish to have sport mingled with rudeness." Finally, in the prologue spoken at court to Elizabeth herself, Lyly concluded by writing that "as in the ground where gold growth, nothing will prosper but gold, so in your Majesty's mind, where nothing doth harbor but virtue, nothing can enter but virtue." Lyly's insistent emphasis on the morality of literature is entirely characteristic of his era. Recent critics have sometimes found his works more morally ambiguous than they may seem at first glance, but no one can doubt that morality of some sort was a chief concern of Lyly's writings.

Lyly's prominence as a dramatist writing partly for the court shows that not all Elizabethans, by any means, were as hostile to drama as a very vocal minority were. The queen herself took an interest not only in Lyly's writings but also, at one point, in promoting his career. Unfortunately, nothing ultimately came of his hopes for an official position, and in a sad petition to the queen, written a few years before his death, he dejectedly wrote, "Thirteen years your Highness' servant, and yet nothing; twenty friends that though they say they will be sure [i.e. reliable in helping to promote his career], I find them sure to be slow; a thousand hopes, but all nothing; a hundred promises, but yet nothing." He died, a widower, under the pressure of heavy financial burdens.

GEORGE PEELE

George Peele (1556–96) was the son of an accountant most famous for writing books about accounting (that also included poems), yet the elder Peele also wrote dramatic entertainments commissioned by the City of London. He taught writing and math at an important orphanage and school sponsored by the city and was able to send George to study at Oxford University when the boy was still in his very early teens. Already as an undergraduate, George had translated a play by the ancient Greek dramatist Euripides, thereby exemplifying the strong interest of most educated Elizabethans in classical literature. Eventually he earned an M.A., but by 1581 he seems to have become involved in the developing London theatrical scene. An early prose work dealt with the legend of Troy. This was a favorite subject of many Renaissance English writers, because the English were supposed—inaccurately—to be descended from the ancient Trojans.

An early play, *The Arraignment of Paris* (1581), dealt with yet another favorite classical legend while also featuring the kind of pastoral setting so popular in so much other literature of the time. This play was performed at court before the queen and was, indeed, intended to praise her virtue and her wisdom, as was true of much Elizabethan literature. Peele seems for a time to have found a supportive patron in the Earl of Oxford, a highly influential courtier who was keenly interested in literature. Peele's career, then, exemplifies the importance of various kinds of patronage in Elizabethan culture. Meanwhile, the Earl of Oxford's willingness to encourage Peele shows, once more, that some of the most powerful people in the country found little to object to in contemporary drama. It was often welcome at court and endorsed by high-ranking figures there, including Elizabeth.

Peele also wrote various celebratory pageants commissioned by the City of London, thus illustrating another kind of patronage important to numerous writers. Many significant dramatists wrote pageants, although such works tend to receive far less attention today than Elizabethan writings for the public stages. Also typical were Peele's dramas on recent and past English history—the former reflected in his patriotic play *The Battle of Alcazar* ([1586] about English conflict with Catholic Spain), the latter in his drama *Edward I* (1590). Meanwhile, his play *The Love of King David and Fair Bathsabe* (1587) obviously shows the Bible's influence on much fundamental thinking of the period, while his drama *The Hunting of Cupid* ([1586] from which only fragments survive) exemplifies the standard Elizabethan interest in questions of proper kinds of love. However, the play by Peele that provokes the most interest today is *The Old Wives* [sic] *Tale* (1588), a comedy rooted in English folklore and featuring various fairy-tale elements. The diverse topics of Peele's plays make him in some ways one of the most inventive of the early Elizabethan dramatists.

Although Peele in his own day was sometimes accused of dissolute living, modern scholars have offered more nuanced accounts of his life. In any case, his avowed commitment to the standard Elizabethan doctrine of using art to teach morality is clear from various sources. The subtitle of *Edward I*, for instance, declares the play to be "A Warning-Piece to England Against Pride and Wickedness," and it also announces that the play will illustrate "the fall of Queen Eleanor, wife to Edward the First, . . . for her pride," which was punished "by God's judgments." Indeed, some critics have even seen Eleanor as a female vice figure, while the opening scene of Peele's *The Battle of Alcazar* suggests the play's moral emphasis by presenting "devils coated in the shapes of men." However Peele actually lived his own life, in his art he was publicly committed to promoting virtue.

CHRISTOPHER MARLOWE

Aside from Shakespeare himself, Christopher Marlowe (1564–93) is probably the English Renaissance dramatist who commands the most attention from scholars and who arouses the most curiosity among a wide range of readers. Partly this interest in Marlowe results from his position as perhaps the most talented dramatist who preceded Shakespeare; partly it results from his status as an important innovator in the history of drama; but partly it also results from the sheer mystery and complexity of his personal life and the shocking nature of his early death. Particularly intriguing is the question of his religious opinions. Was he, as some evidence suggests and as some contemporaries claimed, a thoroughly skeptical atheist who expressed contempt for Christianity in highly cynical language? Or was he, as some modern scholars have argued, an orthodox Christian whose writings effectively promote

A 1585 portrait said to be of Christopher Marlowe. This was painted by an unknown artist and is currently hanging in Corpus Christi College at the University of Cambridge, England.

Christianity? Was he, on the one hand, a radical who really served no one but himself? Or was he, conversely, a valuable, willing government employee—perhaps even a spy—who served the established church and the political establishment in general? Finally, was his sudden death in a brawl—he was stabbed above the eye and died instantly—completely unpredictable, or was he deliberately assassinated? Many confident answers have been given to all of these questions, but often those answers are contradictory. Marlowe's life is likely to remain mysterious, and the ultimate purpose of his works—especially their moral purpose—will probably be endlessly debated.

What were Marlowe's own declared intentions in his plays? How did he present himself to his first audiences, and how was he represented by his publishers to his initial readers? Prefacing the first part of his famous *Tamburlaine the Great, Part I* (1587) is an address by the printer "To the Gentleman Readers and Others that Take Pleasure in Reading Histories." The printer commends the "eloquence of the author" and the "worthiness of the matter." Meanwhile, Marlowe himself, in the prologue, proclaims stylistic novelty, asserting that he will reject the "jigging veins of rhyming mother wits, / And such conceits as clownage keeps in pay," offering instead far more lofty, elevated diction. In the sequel to this work, he promises to show how "death cuts off the progress of [Tamburlaine's] pomp," revealing how "murderous fates throws [sic] all his triumphs down." It is easy, then, to read the story of the great warlord as finally a story of pride punished. Tamburlaine is often seen as an instrument used by God to scourge others' sins, only to be finally punished for his own. Indeed, Tamburlaine's final words are "Tamburlaine, the scourge of God, must die."

Perhaps the play by Marlowe that lends itself most obviously to a Christian, moral interpretation is his best-known work, *Doctor Faustus* (1588), which can be read as rebuking foolish pride and as a warning against numerous sins. Faustus, talented and with enormous potential for good, instead makes an extremely shortsighted bargain with the devil and, after refusing to repent, is finally dragged into hell. Ultimately, he refuses to seek God's mercy, although he does seem to genuinely feel, and also deeply comprehend, the stupidity of his earlier conduct. A "Chorus" finally pronounces a conventional moral that, in the eyes of many readers, perfectly explicates this tragedy's meaning:

> Cut is the branch that might have grown full straight . . . .
> Faustus is gone: regard his hellish fall,
> Whose fiendful fortune may exhort the wise,
> Only to wonder at unlawful things,
> Whose deepness doth entice such forward wits
> To practice more than heavenly power permits.

Controversy about Marlowe's career and writings will probably never cease, but anyone who wishes to see him as a spokesman for basic Elizabethan moral values will always be able to point to words like the ones just quoted.

ROBERT GREENE

Robert Greene (1558–92) is far less well known today than Marlowe is, but in his own time he was one of the most visible—perhaps even notorious—writers among all the Elizabethans. The list of his published works, mainly prose pamphlets, is extremely long; he was definitely one of the first people in England to earn his living almost entirely by writing for the printing press. Yet Greene became famous in London not only for his literary achievements but also for his alleged lifestyle. In work after work, he presented himself and his fictional characters as prodigal sons who had learned the errors of their early mistaken ways, ultimately achieving a deeper moral wisdom. Greene also frequently depicted the underbelly of life in Elizabethan London, particularly that of its petty criminals. Although the ostensible purpose of his writings about crime was to warn potential victims, it was only natural for many readers, in his own day and later, to associate Greene with the disreputable conduct he so often described. Some critics believe that Greene's writings

Woodcut showing Robert Greene writing at his desk from the 1598 pamphlet *Greene in Conceipt*. Robert Greene alludes to Shakespeare in his 1592 *Greene's Groatsworth of Wit*. (Woodcut by John Dickenson)

actually gave "respectable" readers a chance to experience, if only vicariously, the immoral behavior his writings frequently depict and ultimately denounce. In particular, some readers believe that Greene presents his criminals in ways that suggest some sympathy with their cleverness.

Although Greene may have had a hand in composing more plays than we can identify today, most scholars believe that he definitely wrote *Alphonsus, King of Aragon* (1586); *The History of Orlando Furioso* (1591); *Friar Bacon and Friar Bungay* (1589); *The Scottish History of James IV* (1593); and *A Looking-Glass for London and England* (1587). *Friar Bacon and Friar Bungay*, perhaps the most famous and popular of Greene's plays, appeals to the common Elizabethan interest in magic (also apparent in Marlowe's *Dr. Faustus* [1588]), just as it also explores such popular themes as romantic complications, the need to control one's passions, and the ultimate importance of devotion to God. The play ends happily, with double weddings and with a prophecy of England's joy under the future reign of Elizabeth. Ultimately, then, this drama promotes morality, devotion to God, and sturdy English patriotism. In all these ways, it is highly typical of its era.

James IV is not a straightforward history play. Instead, it celebrates womanly virtue and courage, condemns royal irresponsibility and evil, and indicts courtly flattery, parasitism, and murderous intrigue. Ultimately, its evil characters are either punished or reformed. The king rejects his early sins and youthful pride, reunites with the good wife he had tried to murder, and orders the execution of the parasites who had encouraged and carried out his evil schemes. The play, in other words, resembles many other Elizabethan dramas by emphasizing the rewards of virtue and the reprehension of vice.

In writing *A Looking Glass for London and England*, Greene collaborated with another prolific author, Thomas Lodge, an admirer of Sir Philip Sidney and a satirist of contemporary moneylending. Lodge had also in 1579 defended drama against the attacks of Stephen Gosson. He offered the standard argument that good literature uses pleasure to teach wisdom. Although Lodge was willing to admit that drama was sometimes misemployed, he concluded that "sure it were a pity to abolish that which hath so great a virtue in it because it is abused." *A Looking Glass*, accordingly, presents and rebukes numerous sins, both those of the powerful and those of more common folk. Rooted explicitly in the biblical book of Jonah, the play has been likened to the blatant medieval "morality" dramas so common before the rise of Elizabethan theaters. Both Greene and Lodge, then, seem to have embraced the typical Renaissance assumption that drama's main purpose was to teach ethics by providing pleasure.

THOMAS NASHE

Although Thomas Nashe (1567–ca. 1601) was mostly a writer of exhilarating nonfiction, he also composed at least one play, had a hand in another, and did some other, less extensive dramatic writing. He was also, of course, a most vigorous defender of drama during the crucial early period when it most needed defending—when it was under constant attack in print and from the pulpit. Nashe offered, in his support, the voice of a polished, practicing, and variously well-connected writer.

Nashe's support would have been especially welcome because he almost always presents himself, in his published writings, as a champion of morality and an enemy of vice. One of his works, *Christ's Tears Over Jerusalem* (1593), laments the manifold sins of contemporary London. Another, *Pierce Penniless* (1592), uses references to the seven deadly sins to attack contemporary social corruption. When Nashe defends poetry and drama, he defends them in moral terms—as inspiring the young, in particular, to want to do good and avoid evil. Moreover, Nashe nearly always invokes Christian ideas and ideals to support his arguments, and one of his most ardent patrons was the archbishop of Canterbury. He recognized and sanctioned Nashe's talents as a satirical writer to wage fierce rhetorical war against extreme Puritans. They, of course, were as opposed to the traditional church hierarchy as they were to drama. Nashe's works nearly always support political, religious, and moral orthodoxy. Even works that can seem, on the surface, fairly radical (such as his enormously bawdy poem *The Choice of Valentines*) can be read as deliberately Chaucerian in the way they use bad behavior ironically to teach ethical and spiritual lessons through comic indirection.

Works by Nashe that might initially seem to have little to do with morality, such as his treatise on nightmares, usually nevertheless emphasize morality, righteousness, and sin. To say this, however, is not to imply that Nashe lived an entirely untroubled life. Far from it. When the satirical battles taking place in London in the late 1590s became too extreme and too personal, Nashe was one of various writers who saw his satires publicly burned by the authorities. Ironically, Nashe's one brush with the prospect of real punishment for his writings came from his collaboration, with Ben Jonson, on a lost play called *The Isle of Dogs* (1597). The play's precise nature is uncertain, as it does not survive and was immediately suppressed. Allegedly it was lewd, seditious, and slanderous. Nashe managed to flee London before he could be apprehended. Jonson, however, was briefly imprisoned. The play was apparently too daring a satire on political policies or personalities at court. It may have satirized a prominent aristocrat in not easily deniable ways. Still, the fact that Nashe's collaborator was Jonson, who always saw himself as a champion of virtue, is very suggestive, as is Jonson's recently discovered epitaph on Nashe. There he praises his dead friend for wit and talent and says he died as a "Christian faithful penitent, / Inspir'd with happy thoughts and confident." Surely this is how Nashe would have wanted to be remembered, and Jonson apparently found nothing shameful in celebrating his close connection with perhaps the most famous satirist in Elizabethan England.

BEN JONSON

Ben Jonson (1572–1637) was considered by many—and certainly considered himself—one of the most talented playwrights of his time. In his own day his reputation easily rivaled Shakespeare's, especially among the learned. Jonson, indeed, was deservedly proud of his own learning, particularly because he was largely self-taught. His father, a Protestant minister during the reign of Catholic Queen Mary I, died before Ben was born. Nevertheless, the intellectually gifted boy received an excellent elementary education, partly thanks to support from others. After his mother remarried a bricklayer, Jonson was pulled from school to lay bricks. He thus never attended any English university, though he probably would have flourished at that academic level. Instead, he volunteered for military service abroad, killing an enemy in hand-to-hand combat. Back in England, he married, became first an actor and then a writer in the developing English theatrical scene, and soon became a major literary presence. Then and throughout his life, he read voraciously.

In a duel with another actor, Jonson killed his foe but escaped severe punishment by claiming self-defense and by reading a biblical passage (the so-called "neck verse") in Latin. This odd escape clause survived from earlier times, when only priests, who were not supposed to be punished by secular authorities, could read Latin. In any case, this was just one of Jonson's many legal difficulties. Twice he was in trouble for writing plays that seemed overly satirical to certain authorities; another time he was in trouble for allegedly refusing to attend Anglican church services (he had become a Catholic during one of his imprisonments). Jonson was always feisty. He was a man of strong convictions and was almost always ready for a fight. Eventually, however, most of his combats took place in writing rather than on the fields or in the streets.

Many of Jonson's numerous writings are satirical to one degree or another. They mock vice, attack social corruption, and either openly celebrate or implicitly recommend virtue. Jonson, even more obviously than many playwrights, believed that good writing should promote morality. Sometimes he achieves this purpose through clever irony—as in his great plays *Volpone*

(1605), *The Alchemist* (1609), *Epicoene* (1609), and *Bartholomew Fair* (1614)—but in other works he is often less subtle. Rarely, though, are the ethical dimensions of Jonson's writings far beneath the surface. He saw the roles of poet and playwright as greatly significant: A talented and virtuous poet was as important to the commonwealth as a good king. Jonson soon won favor and substantial patronage from King James and many other aristocrats. He was especially appreciated for his royal "masques." These elaborate entertainments combined poetry, music, and dance with spectacular costumes and visual effects. They were usually performed at court, with courtiers participating and with the king, the object of all eyes, watching and sometimes commenting. Jonson, of course, felt

Benjamin Jonson, early nineteenth century copy after a 1617 original (*Original by Abraham van Blyenberch*)

that poetry was by far the most important art form involved, even if many courtiers seemed more interested in the music, dancing, and appealing sights. In any case, James greatly valued Jonson and even, eventually, granted him a royal pension (including wine, which Jonson loved). In 1616, when James published his own massive folio *Works*, Jonson did the same—the first playwright in England to present himself so grandly. Jonson was also heavily involved in preparing Shakespeare's posthumous first folio in 1623. When Jonson died in 1637, his elaborate funeral was attended by many prominent people. Although an early play had landed him in prison, ultimately he had helped transform the status of English drama.

JOHN MARSTON

John Marston (1576–1634), a university-educated writer, also studied law in London at the Inns of Court. His lawyer father hoped his son would follow in his footsteps but was disappointed when John became involved in the theater and began to establish a reputation as a fierce satirist. At first Marston seems to have admired his fellow playwrights, even trying to praise Jonson. The praise, though, was misinterpreted, and Jonson and Marston quickly became involved in an intense wit combat called the "poetomachia." This poets' war eventually damaged both their reputations, at least temporarily.

Neither could easily step away from a fight, and Jonson later boasted that he had actually beaten Marston and taken his pistol. Oddly enough, eventually the two seem to have become reconciled, and it was thanks to later collaborative work with Marston and George Chapman that Jonson was once again imprisoned. *Eastward Ho* (1605), a play accused of mocking Scots and touching on other sensitive political issues, was reported to the authorities, and for a time the playwrights seemed in serious trouble. But thanks in part to help from influential aristocrats, the episode soon blew over.

Like practically all the other famous dramatists of his era, Marston repeatedly claimed or implied that he wrote to teach morality. Many of his claims have already been cited earlier in this book, but further evidence may be worth mentioning. Thus, *Histriomastix* (1598–99) attacks social corruption and praises Elizabeth as capable of restoring the nation's virtue. The play satirizes such vices as pride, vainglory, hypocrisy, and envy, and it celebrates Elizabeth as "Peace's patroness, Heaven's miracle, Virtue's honor, Earth's admiration, Chastity's crown, [and] Justice's perfection." The play is therefore typical of much Elizabethan drama, which often presented powerful people in attractive terms, if only to encourage them to prove worthy of such celebration. Often, to be sure, powerful figures were satirized onstage—King Lear is only one example—but the satire was usually safely distanced from contemporary English monarchs or other aristocrats.

Other plays by Marston satirize various kinds of vices, including usury and pretension in *Jack Drum's Entertainment* (1600); envy, pride, and courtly foolishness in *Antonio and Mellida* (1600); evil in a parent and ruler in *Antonio's Revenge* (1600); foolishness and lust in *What You Will* (1601); and flattery and parasitism in *The Fawn* (1604). Some readers have seen the last of these plays as perhaps satirizing the court of King James and even perhaps James himself, but other scholars remain unconvinced. If Marston implicitly satirized the monarch, however, that possibility only shows how serious he was about using his plays to teach morality, even at the risk of offending the most powerful person in the land. In any case, Marston apparently suffered no ill consequences from this play, which had had to be read and approved by the royal censor before performance. General satire of corrupt courts and corrupt rulers was wholly acceptable. Obviously personal satire—like that in *Eastward Ho*—was far more likely to cause trouble. Attacking vice in broad terms was seen by many (including Marston, Jonson, and Chapman, among many others) as a legitimate part of a playwright's job. Using the stage to score personal points was not, especially if the people attacked were socially prominent. Jonson and Marston might abuse each other in the poetomachia, but any open attack on the royal family or other powerful people was unwise, and thus blatant attacks on the nation's rulers seem almost nonexistent in Elizabethan or Jacobean plays. Ultimately and unsurprisingly, Marston became a priest.

THOMAS DEKKER

Thomas Dekker (ca. 1572–ca.1632) wrote or co-wrote scores of plays, once contributing to 44 dramas in four years. He was also the author of numerous works of prose. He thus exemplifies the heavy emphasis on collaboration among Elizabethan dramatists as well as the involvement of many playwrights in composing works in varied genres. As one of a growing band of professionals who lived mainly by writing, Dekker achieved a huge record of sheer productivity. Some critics consider his voluminous works too hastily composed, but his surviving texts often brim with talent and energy. Most of the plays he worked on are lost—again, a typical fate. Just as most television or movie scripts are not published, the same was true of theatrical scripts in Dekker's era. The surviving Elizabethan plays are just the tip of a massive iceberg that will unfortunately remain forever invisible. Some anonymously written surviving plays may or may not be Dekker's in whole or in part; their precise authorship is always likely to remain obscure.

Like many other dramatists and prose writers of his day, Dekker was especially concerned to mock such flaws as foolishness, irrationality, and sinful or vicious behavior. He was, in other words, often a satirist in a great age of satire. Yet Dekker (again like many of his fellows) wrote in numerous dramatic genres, including comedies, tragedies, history plays, revenge plays, and other common types drawn from many kinds of contemporary and ancient sources. His splendidly funny play *The Shoemaker's Holiday* (1599) shows his ability to root some of his work in the life of London. The play is an early example of the "city comedy" that became a special hallmark of Elizabethan and Jacobean drama. Like many comedies of the time, *The Shoemaker's Holiday* shows true love overcoming various obstacles and harmony uniting distinct social classes.

Old Fortunatus (1599–1600), another play by Dekker, once again celebrates virtue and satirizes vice, and, as was typical of many Elizabethan plays—especially those performed at court—Elizabeth herself is complimented as a particularly compelling example of virtue. *Lust's Dominion* (1600), meanwhile, satirizes uncontrolled passion in a Spanish setting but also involves Moorish characters. The play thus illustrates the tendency of many Elizabethan plays to associate vicious behavior with foreign lands, including Spain and France but especially Italy. Meanwhile, Dekker's *The Whore of Babylon* (1606) attacks

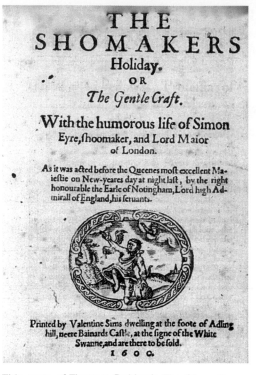

Title page of Thomas Dekker's *The Shomakers Holiday* (or *The Shoemaker's Holiday*), printed in 1600.

Roman Catholicism, while *The Honest Whore*, parts I and II (1604), depict a fall from virtue followed by sincere repentance.

One of Dekker's feistiest plays was *Satiromastix* (1601), which aided Marston in his extended mudslinging match with Jonson. *Satiromastix* mocks Jonson so devastatingly that it seems to have brought the combat to an abrupt end, with Jonson licking his wounds and soon turning (briefly) from satiric comedy to satiric Roman tragedy in his play *Sejanus, His Fall* (1603). Another playwright—probably George Chapman—seems to have had a hand in that text, but when it was published, Jonson deleted his partner's work and claimed the play as wholly his own. Jonson, unlike Dekker, preferred to work by himself.

BEAUMONT AND FLETCHER

Francis Beaumont (1584–1616) and John Fletcher (1579–1625) are almost always mentioned together, as if they were an enduring collaborative team and as if Beaumont were the more prominent. They did indeed collaborate on various significant and successful plays and helped ignite an interest in tragicomedy during the final decade of Shakespeare's lifetime and beyond. Yet Beaumont eventually abandoned playwriting and soon died, while Fletcher actually wrote most of the surviving plays from the "Beaumont and Fletcher canon." Beaumont contributed to approximately one-fifth of the 54 plays often associated with his name. Fletcher is therefore actually the more important of the two, especially because he essentially succeeded Shakespeare, after the latter's death, as principal playwright for the King's Men.

Beaumont, however, would be significant if he had done nothing other than write *The Knight of the Burning Pestle* (1607), an inventive and hilarious comedy. Almost from the very beginning, the play is laugh-out-loud funny, although its highly unconventional humor was apparently not understood at first. In any case, the play demonstrates the important place of comedies on the Elizabethan stage. Theatergoing was often associated with laughter and mirth, and few plays are more mirthful than this one, in which actors pretending to be ignorant of drama are planted in the audience and keep interrupting—and indeed actually taking over—the play they are supposedly there to watch. Sometimes the play is seen as a satire on common London citizens, but the overall tone is one of hearty good fun.

Ironically, Fletcher's most famous work, *The Faithful Shepherdess* (1608), a celebration of chastity, also failed when first performed. In retrospect, however, it helped arouse the Jacobean appetite for tragicomedies, an appetite that even Shakespeare sought to satisfy when authoring his late "romances." Beaumont and Fletcher, in turn, were often strongly influenced by Shakespeare's writings, and

Portrait of John Fletcher, co-writer of *Henry VIII* and *The Two Noble Kinsmen*, by an unknown artist.

Fletcher collaborated with Shakespeare on three plays: *The Two Noble Kinsmen* (1613), *Henry VIII* (1613), and *Cardenio* (1612–13; now lost). The fact that the King's Men made Fletcher their main dramatist after Shakespeare retired speaks well of their confidence in his abilities. A few weeks before Shakespeare's death in 1616, Beaumont had also died, and so Fletcher had permanently lost two of his most important collaborators. Yet he remained highly productive until his own death in 1625 (the same year in which King James died). His works, like the works of many playwrights of his era, often have decidedly moral purposes and tones, particularly when they show the unfortunate consequences of pride and unbridled passion. In later decades, Beaumont and Fletcher would be remembered together as two key dramatists of their era, their names forever linked.

THOMAS MIDDLETON

Many scholars of Renaissance drama consider Thomas Middleton (1580–1627) one of the best playwrights of the time. Middleton's father, although a bricklayer, was a gentleman by the standards of the day. He was able to send Thomas to Oxford, where he may have worked on an early published text, a lengthy verse paraphrase of the teachings of the biblical King Solomon, which Middleton dedicated to the enormously powerful Earl of Essex.

Illustrated title page of Thomas Middleton's *A Game at Chess*, published in 1625. The page includes the phrase "as it was acted nine dayes to gether at the Globe on the banks side."

Soon, however, he was in London, composing moralistic and satirical verse that attacked contemporary social corruption. Only when he began writing for the theater, however, did he really begin to make his mark. His earliest theatrical work, in a fashion typical of the time, was collaborative.

When Middleton began writing comedies independently, most had some moralistic slant. *The Phoenix* (ca. 1604), for instance, presents various kinds of corruption and ultimately emphasizes proper ethical conduct. *A Trick to Catch the Old One* (ca. 1605) shows greedy characters punished and humiliated. *Your Five Gallants* (ca. 1605) censures ethical misconduct in London, while *A Mad World My Masters* (ca. 1606) shows how a witty deceiver is ultimately deceived. *Michaelmas Term* (ca. 1606) mocks vanity and materialism, while *The Puritan, or The Widow of Watling Street* (ca. 1606) exposes deceptions, mocks follies, and ridicules hypocrisy. All these plays reveal Middleton's close knowledge of life in London, and all involve some kind of punishment of vice. In both respects they typify the kind of "city comedy" that had become increasingly popular in the first decade of the seventeenth century.

Yet Middleton also left an indelible mark in other genres. His play *The Revenger's Tragedy* (ca. 1606) is one of the darkest, most grotesque, and most effectively gruesome of all revenge plays. It is almost unforgettable. Its depiction of perverse immorality is in some ways as shocking as a well-done modern horror film. Here as elsewhere, Middleton promotes morality by displaying vice—in this case vice that is almost sickening. In another work of this period, *A Yorkshire Tragedy* (1607), he focuses on shocking contemporary murders. Whereas *The Revenger's Tragedy* is set in Italy (as were many English Renaissance plays about vicious behavior), *A Yorkshire Tragedy* shows that there was also plenty of vice much closer to home.

Middleton's growing stature as a playwright is reflected in the strong likelihood that he collaborated extensively with Shakespeare on the latter's *Timon of Athens* (ca. 1605), another dark depiction of social corruption. That Shakespeare trusted Middleton as a partner is, of course, an extremely high compliment. By this time, Middleton had become enormously productive. Later, he continued to produce solid work with predictable regularity, showing himself adept in various genres. *The Second Maiden's Tragedy* appeared in 1611, the same year as his famous comedy *The Roaring Girl or Moll Cutpurse*, as well as the romantic comedy *No Wit, No Help Like a Woman's*. In 1613, another London comedy appeared (*A Chaste Maid in Cheapside*), as did the first of many civic entertainments celebrating city events. By the time of Shakespeare's death in 1616, Middleton had already established an enviable record as a playwright, yet some of his very best works were still to come. Drama, which had had to fight for respect when Shakespeare began writing, was now a widely accepted part of the English cultural scene, and Middleton was one of Shakespeare's most talented heirs.

BIBLIOGRAPHY

Bowers, Fredson, ed. *Elizabethan Dramatists*. Detroit, MI: Gale, 1987.

——, ed. *Jacobean and Caroline Dramatists*. Detroit, MI: Gale, 1987.

Chambers, E. K. *The Elizabethan Stage*. Vol. IV. Oxford: Clarendon Press, 1923.

The Early Modern Drama Database. http://homepage.mac.com/tomdalekeever/earlymodern.html

Erne, Lukas. *Shakespeare as Literary Dramatist*. Cambridge: Cambridge University Press, 2003.

Gurr, Andrew. *Playgoing in Shakespeare's London*. 3rd ed. Cambridge: Cambridge University Press, 2004.

——. *The Shakespeare Company, 1594–1642*. Cambridge: Cambridge University Press, 2004.

——. *The Shakespearean Stage, 1574–1632*. 3rd ed. Cambridge: Cambridge University Press, 1992.

Kastan, David Scott, ed. *A Companion to Shakespeare*. Oxford: Blackwell, 1999.

Kinney, Arthur F. *A Companion to Renaissance Drama*. Oxford: Blackwell, 2002.

Klein, David. *The Elizabethan Dramatists as Critics*. New York: Greenwood, 1968.

McDonald, Russ. *The Bedford Companion to Shakespeare: An Introduction with Documents*. Boston: Bedford/St. Martin's, 2001.

Pollard, Tanya, ed. *Shakespeare's Theater: A Sourcebook*. Oxford: Blackwell, 2004.

Rivers, Isabel. *Classical and Christian Ideas in English Renaissance Poetry: A Students' Guide*. 2nd ed. London: Routledge, 1994.

Shakespeare, William. *The Riverside Shakespeare: The Complete Works*. Ed. G. Blakemore Evans. 2nd ed. Boston: Houghton Mifflin, 1997.

Sidney, Sir Philip. *An Apology for Poetry: or, The Defence of Poesie*. London: T. Nelson, 1965.

Thorp, Willard. *The Triumph of Realism in Elizabethan Drama, 1558–1612*. Princeton: Princeton University Press, 1928.

Wells, Stanley. *Shakespeare and Co.: Christopher Marlowe, Thomas Dekker, Ben Jonson, Thomas Middleton, John Fletcher, and the Other Players in His Story*. New York: Vintage, 2008.

Wells, Stanley and Lena Cowen Orlin, eds. *Shakespeare: An Oxford Guide*. Oxford: Oxford University Press, 2003.

Wickham, Glynne, Herbert Berry, and William Ingram, eds. *English Professional Theater, 1530–1660*. Cambridge: Cambridge University Press, 2000.

INDEX